TAKE THREE

A Life-changing Journey around Northern Spain

JUSTIN WAINWRIGHT

Text copyright ©2020 Justin Wainwright

The author has asserted his moral right under the Copyright, Designs and Patents Act, 1988, to be identified as the author of this work.

All rights reserved. No part of this publication may be reproduced, stored in a retrieval system, or transmitted, in any form or by any means, without the prior permission in writing of the publisher.

1

We were chatting in a cafe near Blackburn market one rainy June afternoon.

"Take us three," Diego said. "I'm going, Frank's come back, and you're out of... between jobs. Everything's fluid in this life."

"In this vale of tears," I said.

"You'll soon find a job, Justin," said Frank, a forty-five-year-old returnee from Spain.

"Whenever you want, really," said Diego, a thirty-four-year-old Spaniard who was about to go home after nine years in sunny Lancashire.

"I know, but I don't want to find one just yet," said I, Justin, a forty-six-year-old jobless, childless divorcee. "For once in my life I've got time and money at the same time, so I want to go somewhere this summer."

Diego smiled. "Come to Ólvega. I'll be there in a week. I can't wait."

"Yes, I'd like to see this marvellous place you've been telling me about for years, but... well, I don't just want to hang around there while you're working."

"Working, me?" Ha, no chance of that for a while. I've been sweating my balls off ever since I came here, so I'm going to take it easy this summer. Come over and we'll take a trip somewhere."

"All right. Where to?"

"Oh, the whole of the north of Spain is beautiful."

"I only went up north once," said Frank. "On a skiing trip to the Pyrenees. I remember the off-piste part of it best, or rather the après ski."

"Pissed?" I said.

"Naturally."

Frank, I ought to point out, is what is nowadays known as a recovering alcoholic, though he refers to himself as a reformed drunk. Early one morning as he lay on a park bench in Almería after an especially heavy session, he found himself beseeching God to release him from the shackles of his growing addiction. He hadn't prayed since his schooldays, but found that God soon worked in a singularly mysterious way. Rather than helping him to quit the booze, He visited a fatal heart attack upon his estranged father, resulting in a handsome and unexpected inheritance. The still dissipated Frank hotfooted it back to Darwen, near Blackburn, to claim the loot and, it appeared, set about making short work of it.

Enter his old friend Justin – nine months before the current conversation that I'll get back to in a moment – to share a night of beery cheer around our old haunts in Blackburn. I immediately perceived that he was knocking them back like nobody's business and later, as I propelled him towards a taxi, he told me about the desperate prayer that had been answered in a way seemingly designed to leave him in Satan's hands before too long. My role in his recovery was merely to tell him not to be such a bloody fool and to see his doctor, who first scared the pants off him, then prescribed some counselling. In the group sessions he saw the fate that awaited him if he didn't knock it on the head, so he did, just like that, and had abstained ever since.

"You should come to Spain with Justin," said Diego, who had only known the sober Frank.

"Hmm, yes, while I'm still a man of leisure I guess I ought to make the most of it, and I would like to see Spain again through clearer eyes. How would we travel?"

"A mechanic friend of mine is sorting out a car for me now. We could camp and stay in cheap hotels. We could visit a couple of people I know too."

"Frank, if you go back to Spain, won't you be tempted to… well, return to your old ways?" I said.

He tipped back his head and peered down his narrow nose. "Definitely not. Since my prayer was answered, properly answered, I've had no desire to touch a drop. I'm not one of these hopeless alkies who can't stop thinking about it, you know. I just got overfond of the stuff and had to give it up."

"There are so many excellent wines in the north," said Diego. "You'll be able to have the odd glass, won't you?"

He shook his head. "Afraid not. Although I'm not a hopeless alky, my brain might react unexpectedly, or so I've been told, so I shan't be touching a drop ever again, just in case."

I recalled his red, bloated face of only a few months ago. "Yes, that's the best way. Me and Diego aren't big drinkers anyway."

Diego chuckled. "Speak for yourself, but I'll do my partying before you come. Yes, we'll enjoy a long, healthy summer on the road, seeing the sights and meeting people. After that we'll all be ready to get back to work, I hope."

"What will you do?" I asked him.

"Oh, there's plenty going on in Ólvega nowadays. I came here because of the crash, but I'd have gone back a long time ago if it hadn't been for Emma," he said, referring to the girlfriend who he'd finally broken up with, partly because she refused to contemplate ever going to live in Spain, preferring the joys of her native Blackburn. "What about you two?"

"I'll soon find another bookkeeping job within half an hour's drive of here."

Frank grinned. "Shame that last place went bust, eh?"

"That wasn't my fault, and I refused to cook their books. What will you do? I don't think there's much call for under-qualified English teachers around here."

"Oh, I don't know yet. My finances are on a knife's edge."

"But I thought you were pretty flush now?"

"I am. The thing is, if I live frugally I won't have to work much, so if I wish I can live my dream, as long as I do it on a budget."

I nodded and glanced out of the misty window. Diego began to fiddle with his phone. Frank had managed to stay off the subject of his new hobby for half an hour, but I feared that this rare hiatus was about to end. I was right.

He grinned and his blue eyes sparkled. "If I come I'll bring my gear, of course. I think the Spaniards will be more willing to participate than the miserable sods around here, present company included. Yes, I'll adapt my scripts and write some new ones. In a beautiful setting with a few spirited people I'll finally be able to begin to turn my dreams into reality. Another cup of tea?"

"I have to be off soon," said Diego.

"Me too."

Frank strode over to the counter anyway.

Diego sighed. "I forgot about that."

"I didn't. Wherever Frank goes, his blasted camera goes too."

He smiled. "Oh, I don't mind. It's a good way to meet people."

"Or scare them off."

I'd better explain. Frank had been a film buff since his teens, and before he went off to Spain at twenty-nine he used to wax lyrical about the joys of movies by the likes of Fellini, Bergman, Godard, Buñuel, Kurosawa and other international directors. This wasn't so bad, because apart from having to watch a black and white film with subtitles now and then, my lack of interest precluded too many boring lectures about the true art of cinema, as opposed to the trash for the masses that Hollywood (and Ealing, Pinewood etc.) usually produced.

On coming into money and becoming sober, however, he'd decided that it was time to launch his own film-making career, so he'd splashed out a couple of grand on a posh video camera and sundry accessories. His closest old friend, namely me, was cajoled into doing all sorts of silly things so that he could get some practice, but when he cast me in the starring role in his first short film I firmly put my foot down, insisting that I had neither the talent nor the desire to appear on the silver or any other kind of screen. After failing to persuade his new pal Diego or anyone else to perform in his rather pretentious little drama, he'd resigned himself to scriptwriting and filming things whenever he got the chance, until he final met a few willing thespians, including his muse, with whom he felt destined to cross paths before long.

As he'd got chatting to the pretty girl behind the counter I feared that he might have her in his sights. Diego and I watched our lanky, balding friend as he prattled and gesticulated to the poor, unsuspecting lass.

Diego sighed. "I suppose he could make a travel documentary on our trip."

"Oh, God, no. That'd be even worse. He'd be at it all day, every day. Besides, it's a proper work of art that he wants to make, or so he claims."

"Oh, let's not worry about it. He can't take much stuff on the plane anyway."

"He doesn't need much stuff to make a nuisance of himself. Just his camera, a tripod, and a mic that he'll pin on anyone who stands still for too long."

"He might attract a few single women on the campsites. Then while he's giving them his spiel we can move in."

"Hmm, it's about time I got a bit of action. Since me and Julie split up last year I haven't had a single date. Maybe I'm getting too old."

"Rubbish. You're fit and you've got all your hair and teeth. What more do they want?"

"I don't know. I haven't had the chance to ask."

"Well, I'm going to find myself a good Spanish wife before long. Emma didn't want kids, but I do."

"I wouldn't mind, but I'll have to get a move on. I'll be fifty in four years."

He chuckled. "Spanish women like older men."

"Er, I'm only coming for the summer, Diego. I can't do bookkeeping in Spain anyway."

He grasped my arm and squeezed it, him being a tactile Spaniard. "Who knows what the future will bring, Justin? Come with an open mind."

"Well, at least I haven't got a house to worry about," I said, as I'd been back in my old bedroom at my parents' house since my separation.

Frank returned with three mugs in his hands and a frown on his face.

"No luck?" I said.

"Bah, when I mentioned doing a screen test I think she thought I was some sort of pervert. People here are so… so inhibited. I'm not sure I'll ever get used to it after fifteen years in Spain." He placed the mugs on the table. "When do we leave?"

"I fly back next Thursday," said Diego. "Give me a week to catch up with my family and friends, then come whenever you want. I haven't been back since last summer. My mum will want to spend some time with me."

"Ah, madre solo hay una," said Frank. I understood this to mean that we only have one mother, but when they started jabbering away in Spanish I soon lost the thread, despite Diego having taught me quite a bit during the eight years since we'd met in a lift. I'd been to see a client, being self-employed at the time, and Diego had just repaired the lift and was trying it out. Being an uninhibited Spaniard, albeit a lonely one back then, he'd invited me to coffee at the same cafe we were now sitting in and we'd hit it off right away.

"Perdona," I said, as I knew that much. "I fear that the language barrier will be a, er... barrier for me there."

"We'll speak English to you," said Frank.

"And simple Spanish," Diego said in Spanish.

"But when we're with other people I'll feel like a spare part."

Diego squeezed my arm again. "No, you won't. It's thanks to you that I speak good English, as no-one else ever corrected me, not even Emma." He turned to Frank, who hadn't had the pleasure of meeting his pretty but rather obtuse ex. "She thought it was cute the way I said silly things all the time. Can you believe that?"

"Yes."

He turned back to me. "Anyway, I feel that I owe you one, so I'll teach you as much as I can."

"So will I," Frank said in Spanish. Diego had told me he spoke it fluently, so all the time he'd spent in the bars of Madrid, Seville and finally Almería had obviously paid off.

"But if you study a little before you come, it'll help, of course," Diego said.

"OK, I'll start watching some of those YouTube tutorials you told me about."

"Good man."

Over our second cup of tea we talked flights, tents, routes and objectives.

"I want our trip to be a total reconnection with my country," said Diego. "I'll never live anywhere else again, no matter how bad the economy gets."

"I want to reconnect with Spain too," said Frank. "But it's going to be very different for me without my helpful but ultimately treacherous friend, alcohol."

I thought about his new and potentially tiresome friend, the video camera.

"What about you, Justin?" Diego asked.

"Eh, what?"

"What do you wish to achieve on our trip?"

"Change," I said off the top of my head. "I feel like a change."

Frank donned his philosophical expression. "Spain changes everyone, for better or worse, but after spending time in the real Spain you'll never be the same again."

Diego nodded. "And for me the north is the real Spain, but of course I'm biased."

"I can hardly wait for this metamorphosis to take place," I said with a touch of well-concealed cynicism.

"That's the spirit," said Diego.

2

The very next day Frank and I booked one-way flights from Manchester to Bilbao for the last Friday in June, a week after Diego's return to his home town of Ólvega in the province of Soria. On the plane I begged Frank not to bore everyone to tears with his movie-making aspirations.

He patted the camera bag at his feet. "Of course not. I'll just take photos of the places we visit."

"Good idea."

"And only think about filming when we stay somewhere for any length of time."

"Oh, I should think we'll be constantly on the move."

"Unless I decide to make a documentary film."

I looked away and winced. "Er, what will that entail?"

"Asking people pertinent questions and recording their responses." He unzipped his bag and took out his camera, as he hadn't seen it for a couple of hours. "This little beauty will open doors for us, you know."

"Right. What kind of doors?"

"I'm not sure yet, but Spaniards like being in the spotlight. Filming will be an excuse to talk to folk we wouldn't normally meet. Yes, I think I'll do that." He stroked the camera – a Canon XA15 Professional – before putting it away. "It's nice of Diego to pick us up at the airport. I assume we'll be setting off on our travels right away."

"He didn't say, but I know his town's quite a way to the south. I expect he'll take us there after the trip."

It had been twenty degrees and sunny in Manchester and the pilot announced that it was twenty-three degrees and raining in Bilbao.

"I didn't expect this," I said as we hurried into the futuristic building designed by the famous architect Santiago Calatrava.

"If we'd flown south we'd be sweating already. The north's far better for an active holiday."

"Not if it rains all the time."

"It's just a summer shower."

"Good."

Diego greeted us as if we hadn't seen each other for several years. Despite the rain, his expression was sunny and his olive skin had already darkened. Here's a bit more descriptive data before I go on. Our heights ascend according to age, Diego being about five feet nine, Frank five-ten and me five-eleven. We're all fairly slim, Frank increasingly so since improving his diet, and all have dark hair, though mine is beginning to grey and about a third of Frank's has fallen out, though he insists that most of the bald bit is his noble brow. He's the only blue-eyed boy among us, while mine have been described as hazel and Diego's are dark brown. Enough said.

"How *are* you, Justin?" he said into my ear, as he was hugging me at the time.

"Er, about the same as last week, but glad to be here."

He released me and pinched my cheek. "Still a bit uptight, I see, but that'll soon change once you get into the rhythm of life here. Come on, let's hit the road."

My initial rhythm of life in Spain – my first visit since a holiday to the Costa Brava some twenty years earlier – consisted of hurtling down the southbound motorway at about 150kph in Diego's silver Seat Leon estate. I was glad it was no longer raining and the roads were dry.

"We'll just pop down to Ólvega for a couple of days. My family are dying to meet you both."

"How far is it?" Frank asked.

"Oh, an hour and a bit."

I knew that his town was about 260km from Bilbao Airport, but at our current rate of knots his estimate would be technically correct. As we snaked between green hills the carriageways sometimes separated to traverse especially challenging stretches.

"Ah, how lovely and green!" Frank enthused from the passenger seat.

"Yes, but rather blurred. Can you slow down a bit, Diego?"

"Ah, sorry, yes." He slowed to 130kph, the speed limit. "It's so good to have a decent car at last after driving that crappy Fiat back in Blackburn."

I remarked that it looked quite new and he told me that he'd splashed out on the two-year-old car because he wanted to give the impression that his stay in Blackburn had been a successful one.

"But it was, wasn't it?"

"Yes, I saved a lot, but people must *see* that." He chuckled. "It's like a tradition to come back from abroad and show off a bit. It's expected of you, but the trouble is that a lot people in Ólvega have nice cars. I'm sure I'll keep it for a long time."

After whizzing through the beautiful Basque Country and reaching more open, less verdant countryside, Diego promised that we'd return to visit during our trip.

"Have you planned a route then?" I asked.

"Yes, but only roughly, and we can always change it. We mustn't be constrained by anything. Ha, if we end up in Frank's old home of Almería, then so be it."

"No, not there. I owe too much money in the bars. Let's stick to the north. The south's no place to be in summer."

"That's true," said Diego. "Look at all the vines. Over there is Logroño, the centre of La Rioja wine industry. A pleasant city with some nice buildings, but not as dynamic as Ólvega."

"I thought Soria was a quiet sort of province," said Frank. "I read in *El Mundo* online that a lot of small villages are struggling to keep their schools open."

"Ha, yes, many young families come to live in Ólvega."

"I thought you said it was a small, peaceful town," I said.

"Yes, peaceful and also dynamic. I'll just have time to show you around before dinner."

The landscape became quite monotonous as we motored past a biggish place called Calahorra. We soon left the motorway and entered more undulating terrain, before the plains opened up once more, the fields now planted with cereals rather than vines.

"There it is, there it is!" Diego cried.

"They look like factories," said Frank.

"They are. The town's beyond them, but let's take a look first."

Thus it was that our visit to Diego's home town began with a tour of the industrial estate.

"So, that's a big pharmaceutical company, and over there a distillery." He screeched around a roundabout. "There they make the best golf balls in Spain, and this is a huge transport company with dozens of lorries. I once saw one in Blackburn and it made me feel so proud. Down there they make car parts and over there cured meats. There are a lot of smaller companies too, about twenty-five altogether. Let's have a look at the town now."

Ólvega didn't look much bigger than its industrial estate. We passed some new blocks of flats, then some older ones and a few houses, before he circled a huge eight-storey building.

"What the heck's that?" I said.

"More flats, of course. A lot of the people from the villages end up living in those."

"So is Ólvega a sort of new town then?" Frank asked.

"Oh, no, not at all. We believe it was founded in the fifth century. Look, in that fine building we have two swimming pools, and here's the new sports centre. That big place a bit like a church is the town hall, and down there is the youth centre. Along here in another new building we have the cultural centre. Few of these things were here when I was a child."

"Are there no old buildings left?" I said.

"Of course. We take good care of our heritage."

He drove along a tree-lined street of oldish houses and past a fine church, before nipping through more narrow streets to a stone hermitage.

"It's very old," he said as we passed. "Let's go for a quick drink before going home."

We soon reached a small, pleasant square.

"We come to the old part of town for drinks and tapas when we want to relax and remember what things were like before. That building is the old town hall, but it became too small for such a dynamic place."

He led us to a busy cafe terrace and greeted a few people before we sat down.

"I'll soon introduce you to some folk, but for now let them wonder who my foreign friends are. I think many are asking themselves why I've come back and what I'm going to do, but I'll keep most of them guessing until after the summer."

The waiter brought three bottles of beer, one of them *sin alcohol*.

"So did the economic crash affect the place badly?" Frank asked.

"Not really, but I lost my job at a wind turbine factory which moved away soon afterwards. I earned a high wage, and although there were other jobs, I didn't want to take a pay cut, so I followed a cousin of mine to Blackburn, though he came back a couple of months after I arrived. He was homesick, you see."

Diego hadn't told me this before and I was puzzled. "Hang on, so rather than working in another factory here, you preferred to come to Blackburn to work in a warehouse for about seven quid an hour?"

"Yes, until my English was good enough to get that job repairing lifts." He chuckled. "Here I think we're very proud, maybe too proud. Only my family knows about the time I spent packing clothes on a twelve-hour night shift. Everybody else thinks I always had a good job there." He pointed at his Seat. "I should really have bought a new car, but I've learnt from the English that it's much cheaper to buy a two-year-old one. I prefer to save my money to be able to buy a new flat with goods views of the hills."

As the sun set behind us we sipped our beer and pondered for a while.

Frank broke the silence. "Diego, I don't understand this place at all. What's the population?"

"About 3,600 right now."

"So small? It's little more than a village then."

He tutted. "Ha, does it *look* like a village to you?"

"Only in this square, but how come a small town in the middle of nowhere has so much industry?"

He smiled. "Because of Emiliano Revilla Sanz."

"Who's he?" I asked.

"Frank, have you ever eaten Revilla chorizo and other cured meats?"

"I think so. You get it in the supermarkets, don't you?"

"That's right. Well, Revilla took over his father's little sausage factory in the sixties and in twenty years he went from having two workers to eight hundred. He was also the mayor for many years and always encouraged other businesses to come here. He opened more factories around Spain and made a fortune, then in about 1986 he sold the business to Unilever for nine billion pesetas."

"How much is that in euros?"

"Er, you have to divide by 166."

Frank swiped and tapped his phone. "That's about fifty-four million euros."

"Yes, quite a lot in the eighties," said Diego.

"A handy sum," said I.

"Yes, so then he started buying a lot of property in Madrid. That was his big mistake."

"Why?"

He shrugged. "He was in the news a lot. It was known how much he'd sold his company for. Then disaster struck." He smiled. "Another beer, or shall we go?"

Frank called the waiter.

"Finish the story," I said.

"Well, in 1988 he was kidnapped by ETA, the Basque terrorists. I was only small at the time, but I remember the great consternation in town. They held him for 249 days in the basement of a little house in Madrid, then let him go."

"Just like that?" I said.

"Yes, just like that, after the family had paid a ransom of about twelve million dollars. The terrorists sent photographs of the cases full of cash to the newspapers. So, in Spain he became famous because of the kidnapping, but here he's much loved for encouraging businesses to come. Maybe his high profile helped to convince them, but the council also sold the land very cheaply and we believe Revilla got the roads improved through his many contacts."

This story gave me food for thought, but I noticed that Frank was beaming dangerously. Diego had also learnt to interpret that twinkle in his eyes.

"Let's go, guys. My mother will be waiting for us."

"Diego, I'd like to interview Señor Revilla."

Diego flapped his hand. "Oh, he's about ninety now, and he doesn't live in town."

"Where does he live?"

With the benefit of hindsight Diego and I know that he should have said Madrid, Los Angeles or even Timbuktu, but he told him that the great man resided in the village of Ágreda, a mere seven miles away. He was also foolish enough to mention that he knocked around the town hall quite a lot, as he still held some kind of honorary position on the council.

Frank clapped. "Perfect. Can you arrange the interview, Diego?"

I coughed. "But we're off on our travels soon, aren't we, Diego?"

"Yes, quite soon. The thing is, Frank, Revilla doesn't give many interviews and now he refuses to talk about the kidnapping. A few years ago he visited one of his captors in prison, as part of some kind of, er... healing initiative. The man apologised, but Revilla said afterwards that he could never forgive them. They treated him all right, and even gave him some painting things to help him kill the time, but he was kept in a very small space with just a narrow bed and a toilet. Since that newspaper interview I don't think he's spoken about it, and now he's a very old man." Then Diego made his second mistake. "I think he might give an interview to talk about Ólvega, as he's still keen for the town to expand, but the trouble is that journalists always want to ask him about the kidnapping."

""Oh, but I wouldn't ask him about that," said Frank. "I'm only interested in this fascinating and... incongruous town."

"Yeah, right," I said.

He slapped the table. "Yes, yes, that's what I'll do. Wherever we go I'll try to interview the mayor or some other bigwig. Then when I get home I'll make a documentary. I could call it The Changing Face of Spain or something like that."

At that moment in time this scheme seemed like a lesser evil than him filming the travel documentary that I feared. Rather than annoying us day in and day out, he'd simply shoot off to have a chat with a civic dignitary now and then. I wouldn't even have to go, as I'd be of little use.

"I think the mayor would give you an interview," said Diego. "My dad knows him quite well."

Frank smiled. "Thanks, Diego, but I've set my heart on seeing the sausage magnate."

Diego stood up. "We'll talk about it later. Come on, let's go and meet my folks."

3

Diego's parents lived in a modern third-floor flat on the edge of town with good views of the wooded hills to the east. His father Jose was a thin, unassuming man who had just retired from his job at a kitchen furniture factory. He greeted us politely, before melting into the background while his plump wife Merche made a fuss of us, especially me, as Diego had obviously told them a lot about me over the years.

"Why did you not come to see us sooner, Justin?" she asked me in Spanish after serving the main course.

Frank echoed her words in English.

"I got that," I said to him. "Er, normally different holidays to Diego," I said to her.

"He says you were a very good friend to him when he was alone in Blackbone," she said very slowly and clearly, but Frank's loud and simultaneous translation confused me.

"Er, perdona?"

She said it again and Frank matched her word for word.

"Frank, please shut up. I'll look at you if I don't understand anything."

"Pardon me for breathing."

"Just breathe then." I turned to Merche. "Diego also good friend to me. Very interesting for me Spanish friend in England."

Frank sniggered softly. "There are verbs in Spanish, you know."

"I know," I growled.

Merche smiled. "Well, it is good to have you and Frank here and you must stay for as long as you want."

"Gracias."

"You will both sleep in our daughter Paula's old room. I have put a camp bed in there. It isn't as comfortable as the bed, so you will have to decide who will sleep on it."

"Gracias."

"There's no *way* you got all that," Frank murmured.

"I got the gist. Leave me alone. Ask her something."

He entwined his fingers and cleared his throat.

"But not about *him*, not yet," I hissed, as despite seeing little of Frank for fifteen years, I could usually guess what he was thinking, and vice versa.

"Merche, this lamb is delicious. What is the dish called?"

"Ah, the *caldereta* is typical of Soria. I made it especially to celebrate your arrival. We also make it with beef or pork, but I think it's best with lamb." (Ironically, I've had to enlist Frank's help in reconstructing this and many future conversations.) "I'll make more typical Castilian dishes for you, such as suckling pig, and cod prepared in different ways, and several rice dishes."

I glanced at Diego, expecting him to point out that we were off on our travels before long, but he just nodded and munched on.

"And Diego will show you all the sights around here," she said.

"The industrial estate is very impressive," Frank said.

Jose grunted, probably glad to be out of there.

Merche smiled. "Yes, there's plenty of work here. I'm sure my Diego will find a good job soon, won't you, son?"

"Sí, Mamá, quite soon."

Frank smiled. "This Emiliano Revilla sounds like an interesting man, Merche."

"Oh, yes, he's done a lot of good for the town."

"I'd like to interview him. I make documentary films, you see. I'll show you my camera later."

"He won't give interviews now," said Jose.

"Frank will be able to interview Gerardo, won't he, Papá?" Then to us. "Gerardo's the mayor."

Jose nodded. "Yes, he'd give an interview to an espantapajaros."

I looked at Frank but he studiously ignored me.

"A scarecrow," said Diego. "Gerardo loves being on television, you see. Frank, I think you'll have to settle for an interview with him. He can tell you all about Revilla anyway."

"Hmm, we'll see."

After dinner Diego whisked us off to another bar terrace in the modern part of town. Being a Friday night, there were plenty of people around and Diego waved or nodded to several of them.

"Look how happy everyone is, guys. They've worked hard all week and now they can relax. In Blackburn the pubs were always too crowded for me and the people too drunk. Oh, look at that red Porsche there." The car roared past. "Believe it or not he's a lorry driver. When he's not on the roads of Europe he likes to drive around town."

"Isn't that a bit daft?" said Frank.

"Oh, I don't know. I'm sure he'll settle down soon and then there'll be no more Porsche."

I began to notice the number of sporty cars that appeared more than once.

"So are people a bit materialistic here, Diego?"

He smiled. "Of course, and why not? Some of their grandparents and even their parents had hard lives, so they want to show their success. Many work fifty or sixty hours a week, but flats are expensive here compared to other places in Soria. Ha, in some villages you can buy an old house for twenty or thirty thousand now, but a good flat here costs over a hundred."

"That means that people can go back to their village when they retire and buy a really nice place," I said.

"Yes, I suppose they could, or restore their old house, but few do. My parents are from a little place called Deza. They came here a few years before I was born. My grandmother, my mother's mother, still lives there. She's eighty-four now."

Frank's eyes began to shine. "Can we go and see her one day?"

Diego shrugged. "I went last Sunday, but we can go if you like. The village is dying now. The school closed about three years ago because they didn't have the four pupils needed to keep it open. The year after they had a couple more kids, but they didn't reopen it because they knew they'd probably have to close again the following year. Once a village loses its school it's domed."

"Doomed," I said, as I still corrected his rare mistakes.

"Doomed. Thanks. You know, when my grandparents were young, well over a thousand people lived in Deza, but now there are about two hundred, most of them old."

"What did all those people do?" I asked.

"They slaved in the country. Most of them were very poor. Many came here in the sixties and seventies, so there are probably as many *Dezanos* here as in the village, if you count their children. Yes, Ólvega has given my family and many others a better life."

"But hasn't Ólvega caused some of the villages to decline?" I said.

He shook his head. "Not at all. Not one little bit. They'd have gone much further away, to Barcelona, Madrid, or even to France or Germany. At least Ólvega's success means that people have been able to stay in Soria."

The idea of cheap houses in a quiet village appealed to me. I asked Diego if his parents hadn't considered returning to Deza.

"No way. Here they've got the facilities of a town of twenty thousand, but with the countryside just two minutes' walk away. My mum goes swimming and does crafts at the cultural centre. My dad likes walking and he's started going to the retired folk's social club too. In Deza they'd have none of that."

I smiled. "Perhaps they could build a nice house with a pool there."

"A pool? What for? Here it's only warm enough to swim about two months a year. Can you feel the breeze now?"

"Yes, it's getting chilly."

"I told you to bring a jacket, you dope," said Frank.

"Here we're at over a thousand metres," said Diego. "It snows in winter, though not as much as it used to. When my parents were small, Deza used to get cut off sometimes."

Frank smirked. "Justin mentioned building a house with a pool because he has the mentality of an English expat." I sipped my beer and surveyed the other patrons. "In Almería they love to build their posh chalets and pools, even though it's practically a desert."

"What's wrong with that, if that's what they want to do?" said Diego.

"Bah, I despise the lot of them. They sit there frying themselves to a crisp and make no attempt to integrate. I'm glad I won't see any of *that* lot here in the north."

"You might," I said.

"No chance. They haven't got the initiative to stray more than twenty miles from the Mediterranean coast. A pack of philistines, the lot of them. Thank God there weren't too many in the city. So, Diego, when can we go to Deza to see your granny?"

"Tomorrow, if you like."

I sensed what was coming.

"I'd like to interview her, you see. She'll remember the old way of life that's been swept away in the name of so-called progress. It'll make a fascinating documentary for future generations to see."

I gazed at Diego, attempting to convey that if his granny had no objection to being quizzed by a nosey foreigner, it might be a way of diverting Frank's attention away from Señor Revilla. He winked.

"Yes, yes, I'm sure she won't mind doing an interview. She's a little deaf, but her mind is still clear, though you'll probably find that she'll... well, maybe not answer your questions as accurately as you'd like."

Frank smiled. "Oh, I don't mind that. I'm just interested in what she has to say. Thanks, Diego, I'm looking forward to it."

"Me too," I said. "I'm curious to see one of these villages where nobody wants to live anymore."

"And the interview with your granny will be a good warm-up for the one I'm going to do with the sausage supremo."

He grinned, we sighed, then he went to the loo.

"I'm afraid he's going to be tiresome with that camera of his," I said.

"Hmm, I don't really want him to bother Revilla. They treat him like a saint at the town hall, but he can be bad-tempered and if Frank puts his foot in it, people might say it was my fault."

"Maybe he could just interview the mayor on Monday, then we can be off," I said, as I thought three days in Ólvega would be more than enough.

"Yes, but Gerardo's a busy man."

"Perhaps your dad could call him this weekend and ask him to spare twenty minutes on Monday."

"I'll ask him tomorrow. So, what do you think of Ólvega? It's a fine town, isn't it?"

Another car sped past, tooting its horn. "Yes, it's a lively place."

"And there's more to see besides the town. One day we'll walk to an old iron mine that a lot of tourists come to see, and another day we can climb Moncayo, the mountain to the east that you can't quite see from our flat. It's on the border with Aragón and is over 2300 metres high. There are wonderful views all around from up there."

"Yes, I'd like to do some walking. On our travels I'm sure we'll do a lot of–"

"And we'll also visit the church and the four ermitas… er, hermitages."

"All right."

"And if you want to swim, the larger of the two pools is quite big."

"Will we be going to the beach at all?"

"What? Oh, yes, we'll go to the north coast at some point. Where's Frank got to?"

I sighed. "Probably arranging another interview."

"I'll go in and see."

I sipped my beer and told myself not to be impatient. I was eager to leave the bustling town and hit the road, but Diego was trying to be a good host, so I'd have to bear with him. As for Frank, well, the sooner we got him away from there and among strangers the better. If he upset the mayor of some faraway mountain village it wouldn't matter, as we'd soon be pulling up our tent pegs anyway, but if Señor Revilla expired after his ordeal,

Diego's family might be driven out of town and back to the village I was looking forward to seeing.

A smiling Frank returned, followed by a frowning Diego.

"What have you been up to, Frank?"

"Just chatting to a pretty young lady. I told her she reminded me of Silvia Pinal, a Mexican actress who was in the famous Buñuel film, *Viridiana*. Unfortunately she hadn't heard of her or the film or even of the great Buñuel."

"And unfortunately she's also married, to big Alberto, a meat packer who was staring at him from the bar," said Diego.

Frank shook his head. "Not even Buñuel. What's the youth of Spain coming to?"

I chuckled. "Hey, Diego, maybe we should get him out of town quite soon, before he gets into mischief."

"Hmm, shall we head back? You must be tired."

I allowed Frank to use the proper bed on condition that he kept quiet and let me get to sleep. After making myself fairly comfortable I wished him goodnight.

"Yes, night, Justin." He shuffled and sighed. "What do you think of it so far?"

"It's great. Diego's folks have been really welcoming. I'd like to head off on Tuesday though."

"What's the hurry?"

"We've come to travel, to see lots of places. We can always come back here for a few days afterwards. Goodnight."

"Yes, we can always come back." He yawned. "Night."

"Night."

"I'm looking forward to meeting his granny, and the mayor even more. Diego says his dad'll call him tomorrow."

"Good."

"I'll let him waffle on, then with great subtlety I'll persuade him to line up an interview with the tocino tycoon."

I didn't know what tocino was and didn't mean to ask. "Right."

"The tocino tycoon, eh? I like that."

"Hmm."

"Tocino's bacon."

"Ah."

"Except it's normally really fatty. They call decent bacon bacon, but they spell it b-e-i-c-o-n."

I faked a yawn.

"With him being so old I might be the last person ever to interview him."

I recalled his estranged father's fatal heart attack and wondered if Frank had just called him in order to heal their rift.

"Yes, first granny, then the mayor, then the... embutido emperor."

I groaned. "Tell me what that is, then please go to sleep."

"Cold meat, or cured meat, although the verb embutir actually means to embed, or pack, so I guess it really refers to sausage-type products. Yes, because even though chorizo and things often come ready sliced, they were originally sausages. Hmm, I'd never thought about that before."

I grunted.

"I'm glad to see you're making an effort to speak Spanish."

"Sí."

"I've brought a little sound recorder along, so I might record you when you talk to folk, then we can go over your mistakes afterwards."

"Yes, Frank, if you like, but please let me sleep."

"OK, goodnight."

"Night."

"I didn't bring it with that purpose in mind, of course. Sometimes when filming it's better to record the sound separately, or just to have a back-up. I'll probably use it with the... with Revilla, as I don't want to risk messing up such an important interview."

I pulled the pillow over my head and resolved to speak to Diego about our camping arrangements. I promise not to subject you to many more of Frank's frequent ramblings, but I thought I ought to share that first-night discourse with you – or part of it, as it actually went on for much longer – so that you'll know what I was up against. As I vainly tried to get to sleep I calculated that we hadn't been on holiday together for twenty-three years. I hoped I wouldn't live to regret inviting my garrulous pal along.

4

The next morning after a hearty breakfast we headed south through wooded hills onto a vast plain with just a few trees dotted around between the fields. As we approached the village of Deza the terrain became greener and more undulating, but on spotting the first houses Diego showed none of the enthusiasm he'd displayed the previous day when the factories of Ólvega had come into view.

"Do you feel that your roots are here, Diego, seeing as generations of your family lived here, tilling the soil?" said Frank.

"Not really. It's a dull place, except at fiesta time in September, when hundreds of people come from all around. I think the locals live for the fiestas, as there's little else to live for here."

I looked left. "Wow, that's a huge church up there."

"Yes, they always had money to build churches while the people struggled to survive."

We entered the village proper and I was surprised how well-kept many of the old three-storey houses were, having been led to expect scenes of desolation. Already impressed, I was astonished when we passed what appeared to be an impeccable stone fortress.

"What's that, Diego?"

He sighed. "I'll turn around up here so you can see it."

We climbed out and from the edge of the village we saw two sturdy, castellated towers atop the imposing square building.

"It's a great fort, Diego. Why didn't you mention it?" I said.
"Oh, it's just an illusion."
I rubbed my eyes and looked again. "No, it's still there."
"I mean that it gives a false impression of the state of the village. The village hall is in there now and they also use it for weddings and other celebrations." He sighed. "Outsiders have great feasts there, while the villagers sit in their crummy houses with nothing to do. They say this place was an important fort in medieval times, when it was on the frontier between the kingdoms of Castile and Aragón. I guess nothing's changed. The wealthy in their palaces and the poor folk in their hovels."

"I haven't seen any hovels yet," said Frank.

"Ah, here many live without double-glazing or central heating."

"Hardly anyone has central heating in Almería."

"They don't need it there. Here they do. I pity my grandma in winter, with her smelly gas heaters and the dirty wood stove. We've tried to persuade her to come to Ólvega, but she's too stubborn. She thinks she likes it here, even though she's seen how well we live in our town."

I recalled the speeding, tooting cars, not to mention the great eyesore of an industrial estate, but I kept these reflections to myself.

"Can we go inside?" I asked.

"Not unless you have business to attend to or an invitation to a posh wedding. Come on, I'll show you the pathetic bullring that people find so interesting."

After passing several more attractive houses we reached a roughly circular sunken corral surrounded by stone walls.

"They say the poor villagers had to cut this out of the solid rock. It's supposed to be the oldest bullring in Soria, but now they just use it for the *encierros* in the fiestas, when they run the bulls into it from the streets."

"Is there a bullring in Ólvega?" Frank asked.

He smiled. "There we just have a temporary one constructed every year for the fiestas. It's very expensive, but we can afford it. We have a proper bullfight and also run the bulls through the streets. That's in September too, and it's much better than here. We hire bigger bulls with longer horns."

I looked at the little slice of history hewn from the rock, then something else caught my eye. I pointed at a large stone archway standing alone on the rocky hillside.

"Hey, what's that, Diego?"

"That? Oh, that's what's left of an old Moorish castle or something. Come on, we'd better have a look at the church now that you're here."

The sixteenth century church is plain from outside, but I was astonished by the huge golden altarpiece and the enormous pipe organ.

"This is quite a place, Diego," said Frank as he snapped away with his compact camera.

"Yes, it's not bad."

"Does the church in Ólvega have an altarpiece and a great big organ like that?"

"Our altarpiece is bigger and better. We spent a lot of money restoring the church when I was a boy. Come on, my granny's expecting us."

The night before while I was waiting for Frank to pipe down, I'd pictured Diego's granny as a stooped, shrivelled, black-clad crone, hunched in an ancient rocking chair in the tatty parlour of a tumbledown cottage. In fact, Doña Teresa was a robust, cheerful lady whose sprightliness belied her eighty-four years. Her house was a neat two-storey affair on a narrow street, with a freshly painted facade and a fairly modern interior. I liked it much more than Diego's parents' flat and I sensed that Frank did too. She ushered us into the cluttered sitting room and went to make coffee.

"Shall I help you, Grandma?" Diego said loudly.

"Of course not. Come and fetch the buns in a moment."

We sat around the large dining table and Frank extracted his video camera and collapsible tripod from his rucksack.

"Er, does your gran know about the interview yet?" I asked Diego.

"No, I forgot to mention it on the phone. I'll tell her now." He left the room.

"Don't pressure her, Frank. She's probably never seen a camera before, what with living in this godforsaken village without any mod cons."

He nodded at the large flat-screen TV. "Our pal's a bit biased, isn't he?"

"Just a bit. I'd prefer to live here than in Ólvega. It's got much more character."

"Why don't you then, or somewhere like it? You could do up one of the cheap houses that Diego mentioned, though I haven't seen too many scruffy ones."

"Yes, but there's the small matter of making a living."

He smiled. "Where there's a will there's a way."

Doña Teresa came in with the coffee tray and Diego followed with a plate of buns.

"Granny made these. She likes to keep herself busy."

Frank had placed the camera and tripod by his side.

"Ooh, what's that for?" she said, in Spanish, of course.

"I hoped to be able to film you a little and ask you some questions about your life here in the village," Frank bellowed.

"Don't shout, son. I'm not deaf. Well, I didn't expect to be doing this again so soon."

"What do you mean, Grandma?"

"Only last month they were here from the television, making a documentary about the villages of Soria."

"What about?" Diego said.

"Yes, I heard they were filming at the new hotel and restaurant, so I walked up there to have a look."

With the instinct of a true pro, Frank swivelled the camera and started filming, before sliding a tiny mic across the table and pinning it to the edge of the wooden tray.

"Why were they filming?" said Diego.

"So, there I was, just minding my own business, and a young man asked me if I'd like to answer a few questions, so I said why not?"

"But what was—"

"Shush, dear. Then he pinned one of those things to me and a young lady asked me if I thought it was a bad thing that the school had closed, and I said well of course it's a bad thing, but what can you do if there aren't enough children? Pour the coffee, Diego. Then she asked me if I thought better internet might bring more people to the village, and I said well of course it might, although I'm not well up on those things, but I know the young ones like it, and part of the reason that the Romeros' daughter and her husband went to live in Soria was because of that and as they have two small children that'll be two less for the school, but of course the lack of a school was another reason for them moving away. Help yourselves to the buns. I made them yesterday. Then she asked me if I thought the hotel and the other place they take in lodgers were good things for the village, and I said of course they are, but the people who come are just tourists and don't make much difference to the rest of us, although I suppose they might go to the bar or the grocer's or the bakery. I had a lot more to say, but she thanked me and went to talk to the man who works in the bank, even though he isn't from here. He's from Zaragoza, but he's very helpful. The coffee's going cold, Diego."

"Ah, yes." He filled our little cups.

Frank covered his mouth to clear his throat, then leant over to get nearer to the mic. "So, Doña Teresa, what do you think the future holds for this beautiful village?"

"You'll have to speak up, son."

He repeated the question and she continued her monologue in the same vein. It occurred to me that Frank was getting a taste of his own medicine, but he seemed happy enough to listen while she opined, in a very roundabout way, that with a little new blood the fall in population could be arrested. Deza would never again be the bustling place she'd known as a child, but if the few young families remained and the courting couples also stayed put, she saw no reason why they couldn't keep their grocery, bakery, bar and bank, as people from the nearby hamlets used them too.

"But what work can the youngsters do here?" Diego asked her.

"Oh, they're used to driving to Soria or Alhama or Calatayud by now. We never had that option."

"But there's nothing for the children or anyone else to do here, Grandma."

"What nonsense! They have the swimming pool in summer, and that place to play sports. Don't start telling me how good Ólvega is again, Diego. Not everyone wants to live in such a busy, noisy place." She then turned to me. "Do you like it here, young man?"

Although I'd caught little of her discourse, I understood that, so in my Indian Spanish I told her that I found the village charming, as I also appreciated peace and quiet, before saying a few nice things about Ólvega for form's sake.

"I'll have to edit out that gobbledegook," Frank muttered. "Tell me, Doña Teresa, what words would you use to describe Deza?"

"Have a bun, son."

Diego burst out laughing. "Great answer," he said in English.

"Crap question," I said.

"I couldn't think what else to ask. She's covered just about everything. I'll make some notes next time."

Doña Teresa unclipped the mic and handed it back to Frank. "Now tell me, how long have you boys come to stay for and what are you going to do?"

The YouTube tutorials I'd watched must have helped a bit, because I understood and lost no time in reminding Diego of the reason for our visit.

"We come to travel in all north of Spain. We go in Diego's car and, er... live in tents. We go Tuesday, I think."

"Ah, very good. It's good to travel. I go into Soria on the bus every week with my friends, and we've also been on coach trips for the old ones to Burgos and Palencia and Valladolid."

"Those trips were some time ago, Grandma."

She glared at him. "And Salamanca and Zamora and León."

Frank glanced at Diego, grinned at me, then turned to Doña Teresa "Just about everywhere in Castilla y León then?"

"Yes, and all very cheap. They look after the old folk in the villages, whatever some people might say."

"Have you been to Astorga, Grandma?"

"Oh, yes, when we stayed in León we went to visit. It's a beautiful place."

"We're going there too." He smiled at us. "And we won't be camping."

"Where will we stay? Frank asked him.

"You'll see. Well, Grandma, we'd better be going now."

After kissing us all she saw us out. "Come to see me again when you get back, boys."

"We will do," said Frank.

"And you practise your Spanish, son."

"Yes, Doña Teresa, I practise. Gracias por el café y, er..."

"Los bollos," said Frank.

"How long will you be away for?"

"A long time," said Frank.

I nodded vigorously and glanced at Diego, because besides being in no hurry to leave, he hadn't so much as mentioned the tents and other camping equipment he'd promised to borrow. His brow clouded momentarily, so I decided to broach the subject on the drive home.

On being put on the spot by both Frank and me he confessed to a long-standing loathing for camping.

"When we talked about it back in Blackburn it seemed like a good idea, but when I collected the gear from my cousin and a friend of mine I started to get cold feet. My memories of camping are of being too hot or too cold and of sleeping badly, but that was a long time ago."

"So have you got all the gear?" I said.

"Yes, two tents, three sleeping bags and mats, cooking things, gas, torches, water containers. Everything, I think, except enthusiasm. I also disliked sharing a tent when I used to go."

"We can stay in hotels too," Franks said brightly. "If it looks like rain or we just feel like it."

"But hotels are more expensive. I can't afford to spend a fortune."

"Me neither," I said. "But I don't think you'll be too hot or too cold in a tent right now, Diego," I said. "It should be just right at night."

"Yes, I'm sure I'll be fine."

Frank leaned forward and patted his shoulder. "And me and Justin can share a tent, so you'll have one to yourself."

His face brightened, so I stifled my incipient cringe. "Yes, we'll do that, Diego."

He smiled. "Thanks, guys. We'll go on Tuesday, shall we? The sooner we start, the sooner I'll get over this silly fear of camping, I hope."

"Yes, as long as I manage to see the cold meat mogul tomorrow." He tapped my head. "I thought of that one earlier."

"Well done."

"Do you mean Revilla?" said Diego.

"Who else?"

"Don't get your hopes up. Anyway, you can always see him when we get back."

"He might be dead by then."

"No, men like him go on forever."

That evening we went out for some tapas and met a couple of Diego's friends, plus his sister and her husband. They all seemed to be cast in the same mould as Diego, being very pro-progress and pro-Ólvega. I only really pricked up my ears when his sister Paula, an attractive lady of thirty-seven, asked him if we planned to visit Uncle Abelardo in Fermoselle. Frank told me later that his reply had been rather evasive. He'd said that as Fermoselle was so far away he didn't know if we'd make it, to which she'd replied that Uncle Abelardo was best left well alone. He'd countered by saying that he was family after all, and she'd grudgingly agreed, before changing the subject.

"Fascinating," I said from the camp bed.

"It is though, isn't it? I was going to quiz Diego about him afterwards, but I've a feeling that he's in two minds about going, so I think I'll adopt a softly-softly approach."

"You? That'll be the day. Why don't you just ask him about this uncle of his?"

"Because I'm afraid he'll overthink things and decide not to go. I reckon the best plan is to steer him in that direction, without mentioning Fermoselle, then suddenly remind him of his long-lost uncle. That way he'll feel obliged to take us there. Like he said, he is family after all."

This seemed like needless subterfuge to me, but I knew that Frank enjoyed a good mystery and saw no reason to spoil his fun. I also knew that if I wanted to sleep I'd be well-advised to agree with him.

"OK," I said, before remembering the little plastic box in my jacket pocket.

"So we're off to see this famous quarry tomorrow. It'll be a good walk and I'm looking forward to taking some pictures. I won't take the video camera, as it's a long way and I doubt we'll meet anyone keen to do an interview, although…"

I inserted the earplugs that I'd slipped off to the chemist's to buy that evening; silicone ones designed to shut out over thirty decibels of noise. The faint murmur of his voice helped me to drift off to sleep, but not before I'd resolved to buy another half dozen pairs.

5

The old Petra iron ore mine lies about three miles to the south of the town. We reached it by one o'clock after a sweaty walk across the fields and through a lovely forest of holm oak trees. It's believed that the mine was first exploited by the Romans, or even the native Celtiberians before them, but it was a Belgian company which really got stuck in at the start of the twentieth century and dug out the great chasm that began to fill with water after the mine finally closed in the 1980s. It's the fact that the resultant lake is emerald coloured that attracts so many visitors, according to Diego, although we only saw three more people that sunny Sunday. After eating the sandwiches his mum had prepared, we took a good look at Mount Moncayo in the distance and agreed to climb it when we returned from the trip which Diego was now more enthusiastic about. On the way back we had a look at three of the four stone hermitages, the other one being some way to the west of town, and also visited the church, where we had to concede that the altarpiece was bigger and better than the one at Deza. We all agreed that both churches made Blackburn's modest cathedral look very plain indeed.

All that remained was for Frank to do his interview with the mayor, which Diego's dad had managed to arrange for eleven o'clock on Monday morning. Citing a sudden interest in the more modern installations of the town, I opted to take a look at the sports and cultural centres instead of joining them at the town hall. After the subsequent fiasco I felt glad to have given it a miss, though now that I come to write about it I regret being unable to give you a first-hand account. Instead I'll have to report the version of events which Diego gave me back at the flat, Frank having hurried away from the scene of his crime.

"Oh, I'll be a disgrace after this," he wailed after stumbling through the door.

"I think you mean *in* disgrace, but you'd better tell me what happened."

He shook his head. "And it was all going so well. Gerardo welcomed us into his office and told Frank where the TV crews usually set up their cameras. Frank only had to ask one question and he was off, telling him all about the history of the town, before moving on to all the current developments. He's done it so many times that it was great to listen to and reminded me what a brilliant place this is."

"Did he tell Frank about Señor Revilla?"

"Oh, that's what makes it so annoying. He told him *loads* of things about him, including the kidnapping, so he had no need to bother the man at all. Oh, God, everyone will be pointing at me at the fiestas this year if they find out, and they will, because Gerardo's not likely to keep his mouth shut about a thing like this."

"So what happened?"

"And who'll give me a job here now?"

"Diego, I can't assess the collateral damage until you tell me what happened."

"Right, so we left Gerardo's office and walked along the corridor. Frank looked into another office and saw an old man sat at the desk, so he just marched straight in and held out his hand. Revilla was a bit surprised, but he shook it, so I went in and explained that my English friend had made a mistake. Anyway, he asked after my family – he's like that, you see – and while I was telling him, that prick took out his camera and grinned at him. He wasn't pleased, but you know what a sweet-talker Frank can be.

He said he'd wanted to meet him for ages, as *I* had told him all about him, and that he'd love to film a short interview for his *production* company, the lying git. If I hadn't been there he'd have told him to sod off, so that makes it even worse for me." He covered his eyes and groaned.

I patted his arm. "Tell me the rest, Diego, then you can forget about it."

"Forget about it? I'll not forget this to my dying day. In the old days they'd have stoned me to death for bringing such an... an infidel here."

Due to Diego's histrionics I was beginning to fear that something truly awful had happened, like another fatal heart attack, but it wasn't quite so bad. Frank had asked him a mundane question about his chorizo company and the old man had brightened as he told him how his meteoric success was all down to hard work, great business acumen, etc. etc. Then Frank blurted out, and I quote Diego quoting him:

"What did you think about when you were shut up in that small space for 249 days and nights?"

Revilla gasped, before his wrinkled brown face turned crimson and he began to pant. "Get him out, get him out!" he croaked, so Diego yanked Frank away and pushed him and his camera towards the door, before trying to loosen the man's collar, apologising profusely as he did so.

"You get out too, you son of a bitch!" he yelled, so Diego slouched away and cowered by the door until he was sure the great man was all right. "Get out, I said, and don't come back. How dare you bring that damned foreigner here to ask me a thing like that, you miserable hound!" he said, or words to that effect.

"So you see, Justin, Frank has ruined my reputation in town forever."

"Oh, it's not such a big deal, Diego. When he calmed down he's sure to have realised that it wasn't your fault."

"I might as well go away tomorrow and never come back. If he tells the mayor and the mayor tells everyone, I'll be a persona non grata forever. Oh, my dad'll kill me when he finds out. I think I'll be taking you straight to the airport after our... oh, God! And now I have to go *camping* with the man who's just ruined my life!"

I'd just brought him a glass of water when the buzzer rang. I opened the door and saw Frank. He was smiling, so I placed my hand on his chest.

"Do you know what you've done, you idiot?"

He went on smiling. "Never fear, it's all sorted."

"How?"

"I snuck into an empty office and after Diego had come past looking like a condemned man I went back in and grovelled a bit. I told him I hadn't meant to ask him about the kidnapping, as Diego had warned me not to, but that in the excitement it'd just come out. He cursed me a bit, then he started chuckling and cursed me some more. I looked all humble and I think he enjoyed reliving old times when he could make folk quake in their boots whenever he felt like it."

"So did you part on good terms?"

"He walked me to the door, slapped me on the back, and went chuckling back to his desk, so I'm sure there's no harm done."

"You'd better tell Diego. He's distraught."

"I heard," Diego said into my right ear. "Thank God for that. I should thank you for going back, but you did such a bloody stupid thing that I won't."

"That's all right. It's true that it just slipped out, you know." He smiled and shook his head. "I'll really have to learn to behave more professionally if I'm going to make a go of this documentary business."

"What business?" I said.

"I'm getting a taste for it. It's more exciting than I thought. Maybe there'll be money in it if I develop my own style."

"What, wind everyone up?" I said.

"No, well, maybe a bit. Not till they explode like he did, but controversial questioning is definitely the way to go. I've got some great foot… a great feeling about it." *

"Do what you like outside Ólvega. No, outside Soria," Diego said, his relief so great that he'd forgotten to be angry.

"All's well that ends well," I said, feeling that a trite platitude was in order.

(*I was given a private viewing of the exciting footage later that day. Señor Revilla really did blow his top.)

After our afternoon naps we sorted out our gear and went shopping for provisions. Later we went back to the old square for a final drink and discussed our plans and aspirations for the trip. Rather than moving on every day, we agreed that we ought to choose interesting places to stay and explore them thoroughly.

"That way I think I'll get used to camping more easily," said Diego. "I always hated putting up and pulling down the tents all the time and having to get used to a new place."

"And I'll be more likely to meet people who're worth interviewing."

"And I'll know when to get well out of the way," I said.

"Ah, it's going to be great fun," said Frank. "Just the three of us on the road without a care in the word."

"Yes, I plan to make the most of it," said Diego. "I doubt I'll have more than three weeks' holiday again before I retire. I'm going to find a good job, buy a flat, and meet a nice woman to marry."

"I'm going to have a good think about my future," I said. "The idea of finding another job in Blackburn or Preston doesn't appeal to me much, and if I buy a house there I'll be tied down again."

"Move to northern Spain then," said Frank. "Your money will last for ages in some little village."

"No, Justin must think about his future. He can't do his work here."

Frank slapped the table. "Bah, work! Is that the be-all and end-all?"

"It's the main thing in a man's life," said Diego.

"Well it shouldn't be. It should be a means to an end."

"I agree," I said. "Would you consider living in Spain again, Frank?"

"I think so. Being at my mother's in Darwen was a relief after so many ups and downs, but I can't stay there forever. For a while I associated Spain with my boozing and thought I'd be better off back home, as the pubs are so dire that I'd never be tempted to go out, but now that I'm back here and not at all bothered by other people drinking, I'm tempted to find a nice place and rent a cheap house."

Diego shook his head. "No, Frank, you'll just end up running out of money."

He smiled. "You don't know how much I've got."

"Tell us then, so we can advise you," I said. "I am a bookkeeper, after all."

"All told I've got about £140,000."

"I've got about ninety grand," I said. "Most of it from selling our house."

"So you both need to work," said the rational one. "Frank, you could go to a town or city in the north of Spain and find another teaching job."

I smiled. "He could try to get one in Ólvega."

"No... I mean, yes, he could, but... but the language school is very small. There are also classes at the cultural centre, but they already have a teacher. It's difficult for you here."

Frank chuckled. "Don't worry, Diego, although it's been quite stimulating staying with you, to be honest I'm not all that enamoured of the place."

Diego gasped. "Why not?"

"Well, to use a word that you're fond of, it's a bit too dynamic for me."

"For me too," I said. "I mean, I like it more than Blackburn, but I like Deza more than here."

"Bah, that desolate dump?" A noisy moped hurtled past. "You'd die of boredom there."

Frank then waffled on for a while about how one should know how to make one's own fun and that a couple of friends and a few acquaintances were enough to enable one to have a rewarding social life. As for work, he said, if one could make a few hundred every month there was no need to earn more, as no-one really needed a posh house or a nice car.

"Oh, you have no ambition at all," said Diego.

"That's right, none at all, or certainly not the sort you're thinking of. I admit that I'd like to make my mark one day, but not in the usual way."

"You made you mark today," he muttered.

"The thing is," I said, still searching for some conciliatory words. "The thing is, Diego, that we're older than you, so we see things differently."

"Only ten years or so."

"But those ten years make all the difference," Frank interrupted before I'd got into my stride. "We're in the second halves of our lives now and must consider how best to spend our autumn years."

"Speak for yourse–" I began, but was hushed by a sweep of his hand.

"Do we want, we ask ourselves, to be thrust once more into the hurly-burly of modern life, or would we prefer to live in a tranquil place and gently mellow in a philosophical manner while enjoying the riches of nature that surround us?"

"That's a lot of hot air," said Diego.

"Yes, it is," I said. "But I see his point. Twenty-odd years of commuting to work every day is enough for anyone. At our age you begin to ask yourself if there isn't a bit more to life."

He tutted. "The answer's clear to me. You must both work for at least ten more years, then you can start thinking about taking it easy."

"There's little longevity in my family," said Frank. "Look how my dad popped his clogs at seventy-one, and for all I know my liver might have taken a battering during my drinking days."

"You told me your blood tests were fine," I said.

"Doctor's don't know everything. Then there's the state of the earth to consider."

I fingered the new packet of earplugs in my jacket pocket.

"What about it?" said Diego.

Frank rambled on about the population explosion and climate change and said that he wouldn't be surprised if we weren't all living in infra-human conditions within twenty years.

"Why twenty years?" I said.

"Because that's how long my money might last if I don't make any more. Oh, I'm being a bit pessimistic, I suppose."

"A bit?" said Diego.

"But when things start to go tits-up there'll probably be a war over resources. If it's a nuclear one we'll be better off in rural Spain than England. In fact we should find a place that's far away from any big cities and go and live there."

Diego chuckled. "Maybe where my Uncle Abelardo is. Fermoselle really is in the back of beyond."

Frank winked at me. "Yes, I've half a mind to just hunker down in one of these little villages that everyone's leaving and make my money last for as long as possible."

"We may visit my uncle, but I'm not sure yet."

"Whatever. Yes, I'd make my ground-breaking films and maybe earn a bit of extra cash on YouTube or something."

"Uncle Abelardo was always really nice to me. I missed him after he'd gone."

"Or perhaps I'll write a book about radical downsizing and flog that online."

"But although he fell out with the whole family, I think they're partly to blame."

"Or I could restore a house, sell it to another discerning peace-seeker, then buy another hovel and do that up."

"He never listens," Diego muttered to me.

"We're up for visiting your uncle if you are," I said. "I looked Fermoselle up and it is off the beaten track, but I'd quite like to go."

Frank gazed at the sky, humming to himself.

"We'll see. Maybe I'll call him and see how he is first."

"You do that," I said.

Frank fell asleep before me that night, worn out after his fatiguing day.

6

It was lucky that Diego had bought an estate car, because we were just about able to pull the parcel shelf over all our stuff, so if we visited any large towns or cities it would be concealed from view. In the end we'd allowed him to plan our route – subject to a certain amount of leeway if either of us felt a burning desire to visit any particular place – but he preferred to reveal it to us as we travelled, claiming that this would make it more exciting. After wishing his parents a fond au revoir, we left town just after nine and headed west towards Soria, before bypassing the small city that he said we could visit anytime and taking the N-111 road north. The sun shone as we hurtled across the plain and into greener, more rolling terrain, before joining the motorway near Logroño, a city he said we might as well leave for later.

As the motorway curved north I pointed out that we appeared to be returning to Bilbao.

"No, not so far." He switched on the sat-nav, turned off the sound, and smiled.

"Shall we stop for a break?" Frank said from the back.

"No need."

He soon turned onto a westbound motorway that we left quite soon to take a quiet road which led us past a significant sign.

"Kaixo, Euskadi," said Frank. "That means 'Hello, Basque Country.' Let's stop and have a drink. You can have a Txakoli. That's a typical white wine here."

"Yes, we'll stop soon."

After passing two pretty villages, when a third came into view Frank threatened to leap out of the moving car.

"OK, we'll stop here."

On reaching the first houses of Villanañe he whizzed off up a lane to the right.

Frank growled. "Oh, come *on*, Diego!"

Giggling, he bore right onto a narrower lane, hurtled into dense woodland, and screeched to a halt outside the gates of a campsite. Then he fiddled with his instruments.

"Ha, 226 kilometres in just over two and a half hours. That's at least fifteen minutes ahead of schedule. Hmm, fuel consumption, 4.9 litres per hundred kilometres. That's pretty good considering the speed I was doing. Anyway, this is it."

"I feel a bit dazed," I said. "Why were you in such a hurry, Diego?"

"Oh, I didn't want us to get here too late."

"It's twenty to twelve," said Frank. "We could have stopped off in other places. This is supposed to be a road trip, not Le Mans."

"I wanted us to get a good place to camp. It might take me a while to settle in this first time. The sooner we get the tents up, the sooner I can relax."

Only a Saharan nomad could have settled into our tents after we'd pitched them, because the huge field we'd been assigned had practically no shade at all – just a lot of young and ineffectual trees – and the sun was beating down with a vengeance. The lad who attended us had explained that the plots in the field with lovely big trees had been booked up well in advance. The thirty or so other tents in our field were zipped up and only a handful of cars remained.

Frank and I had pitched our blue three-man dome tent in a slapdash fashion, keen to avail ourselves of the swimming pool, but Diego was far more meticulous with his green two-man tunnel tent, tensing each guy rope as if it were a guitar string. When he'd finally attached the inner tent he took a water container and a cloth inside.

"What are you doing in there?" Frank asked him five minutes later as we sat in the shade of the car.

"I'm washing the floor. I can't stand dirt, you see."

"A bit of dirt never did anyone any harm, my grandma used to say," I said.

"That's why kids nowadays pick up all sorts of infections, because they're not used to it," said Frank.

"Please pass me the bottle of washing up liquid," said Diego. "I've found a stain which could be anything. I knew I should have bought a new one."

I found it, slipped it into the furnace, and told him we'd see him by the pool.

"OK, I won't be long."

The site boasted many park homes and cabins and also catered for a few dozen camper vans, so we found the large pool and the rough grass around it full of folk. The strip of shade provided by trees on one side was fully occupied, so we lost no time in stripping off and plunging into the pool, which must have been heated or fed by thermal springs, as the water was lukewarm.

"Not as bracing as I expected," I said as we waded towards the less crowded deep end.

"This is like a bloody holiday camp," Frank whined.

"That's more or less what it is. The restaurant looked huge."

"And there's a damn supermarket, for God's sake. We shan't get much peace and quiet here."

"I wonder why Diego chose the place."

When he joined us in the water a while later he told us that he'd chosen it precisely because it had excellent facilities and great reviews.

"I thought it'd be a safe bet for our first camp." He looked down. "I hope none of these kids have been pissing in the water."

"Urine's an antiseptic," said Frank. "They used to use it in wartime to clean wounds."

I gave Diego a shove. "So you should have pissed in your tent."

We then started splashing each other until the haughty young lifeguard blew his whistle and scowled at us.

"We can't even have a bit of fun here," Frank muttered. "So what's the plan then?"

We agreed that it was too hot to have lunch at the tents and too soon to start spending our precious cash in the air-conditioned restaurant, so we nipped back to make some tuna butties and headed off into the woods to the west of the site, where we found a delightful stream and many other campers. After moving upstream a few hundred yards we reached a quiet spot and settled down on the grassy bank. When Frank emptied our bottle and refilled it with the crystal clear stream water, Diego said he feared that it might contain microbes.

"Of course it does, but good ones. There's nothing wrong with this *ur* from the Basque hills."

Diego frowned and I nodded.

"I said there's nothing wrong with this *ur*."

"I heard you," I said.

"*Ur* is water in Basque."

"Yes."

"You're probably wondering how I know that."

"I'm guessing that you've looked up a few words to impress us."

"*Ez*."

I nodded.

"*Ez* means no. They also say no for no, but that's probably a modern corruption. Basque might well be the most ancient language in Europe, you know."

"I believe so," said Diego.

"Because they were never invaded, or not properly. Historians reckon they were here for at least thirty thousand years before the Romans turned up, but they were clever enough to get on with them till they left. After that they fought off the Visigoths and whatnot and even the Moors didn't manage to conquer them. It was called the Kingdom of Navarre for a few centuries, then Napoleon steamed in and was a bit of a pain, but they got shut of him and more or less governed themselves till Franco came along. That sneaky devil got loads of Spaniards to move up here to try to dilute them, but they're still very independent."

"That's what's called a potted history of the Basque Country, Diego," I said.

"*Bai*," said our lecturer. "That means yes. I'm sure you're wondering how I know all this."

"I know you're going to tell us."

"It's because of my drinking buddy Karlos who I knew in Seville. That's Karlos with a K, by the way. He's from a town called Ondarroa up on the coast, one of the most Basque towns in the Basque Country, or Euskadi, as he always called it. Everyone speaks Basque there, or Euskara, as he would say. He was working for a telephone company and I think he might be back there now. Shame I didn't bring his number. All the stuff he taught me is coming back to me now. Funny that, isn't it?"

"I haven't heard anyone speaking Basque yet," said Diego.

"Oh, they're all bloody tourists from Spain."

"We're in Spain," I said.

"Try telling Karlos that. Hmm, I wonder if my mum could find his number for me. You'd like Karlos, and Ondarroa wouldn't be too far out of the way."

"Er, would it be wise to meet up with an old drinking buddy, Frank?" I said. "He might trigger something off in that head of yours and make you hit the bottle."

"Nonsense. Anyway, I used to do most of the drinking. He's a lightweight like you two."

We ate our butties with our feet in the stream and Frank drank liberally from the bottle, while I took only the odd sip and Diego wouldn't touch it.

"It tastes a bit strange," I said.

"That'll be the peat or something," said Frank. "It'll do our immune systems the world of good. I plan to drink nothing but this *ur* while we're here, and the odd *kafea*, with a K. That's coffee, of course."

On spotting a flat bit of grass across the stream I said I fancied a short siesta.

Frank tutted. "Not a good idea, Justin. While camping we should rise at the crack of dawn and get to bed at nightfall. That way we'll make the most of the cooler morning hours and won't keep folk awake with our chatter at night."

I argued that if we had naps we could enjoy the cooler hours of the morning *and* the evening. It was about thirty degrees at the time, but the humidity made it feel hotter.

By way of reply he picked up his knapsack and headed off upstream. "Come on, let's find the source of this."

Fortunately Frank was diverted from his quest when after about three minutes we came across a cluster of buildings, including an old, square church and an incongruously new four-storey edifice which looked like a block of flats, but was in fact a *Centro de Espiritualidad*, or spiritual centre. There was a bar alongside it, which Diego and I rushed into to slake our thirst. We both gulped from a large bottle of mineral water, but Frank wouldn't touch the insipid stuff. Later, while drinking our coffees, Frank waylaid a passing nun and asked her what went on in the spiritual centre. She told him that it was in fact a religious seminary where some Catholic priests and nuns lived, in order to be close to the sanctuary and to serve the many small villages in the area. They also received many visits from clerics and other devout people who wished to rest and pray in those beautiful surroundings. The devil in our midst then told her that he made spiritual documentaries and asked her if he could interview her the next day. By way of reply she smiled beatifically, nodded at each of us, and appeared to float out of the bar.

I chuckled. "Bad luck, Frank."

Frank gazed at a party of pious-looking people who passed by before entering the hermitage.

"I need to do some research before I ask anyone else. They have to see that I'm clued up about the place."

"Yes, and not just some random spiritual documentary maker who happens to be passing through," I said.

"I want nothing to do with any more interviews," said Diego. He tapped my arm. "He's bound to upset someone."

"I fear so."

"Nonsense, but I can't just ask a load of inane questions. I must find an angle." He knocked back his coffee. "Let's see if we can find one over there."

We told him we'd join him shortly and watched him stomp across to the sanctuary.

"Another coffee?" I said.

"Yes, I think so."

Diego ordered two more *cortados* and I asked him if we'd be going anywhere else in the Basque Country.

"I planned to drive up to the Cantabrian coast next, but I suppose we could go to Ondarroa if he wants to."

"Let's see how he behaves here first."

A while later we were just about to leave when Frank emerged from the sanctuary with a tall, elderly man. They stopped in the shade to continue what appeared to be a lively discussion, so we watched them through the window. Frank pointed towards the stream, then at the sanctuary, and shook his head. The old man shrugged, placed his hand on his heart, and appeared to speak serenely to our restless friend, who shook his head a few more times, before folding his arms and beginning to nod. Presently the man grasped Frank's arms, before shaking his hand and strolling into the spiritual centre with a saintly smile on his face. Frank scratched his head, picked his nose, and seemed disinclined to move, so we walked over to join him in the shade of the wall.

"Did you find an angle?" I asked him.

"Hmm." He took the bottle from his bag and drank some more stream water. "Ah, that's good. Look, just pop in there and take a look at the Virgin, will you?"

We entered the cool chapel and walked past the pews to a modest altarpiece containing an elaborate carving of the Virgin Mary. Diego crossed himself and we left.

"Right, now let's have a look at the grotto," said Frank.

We followed a few pilgrims to a fenced-in enclosure by the stream where we found a sculpture of the Virgin with the baby Jesus. Diego crossed himself again.

"You don't even go to church," Frank murmured.

"Yes, I do."

"When?"

"Whenever there's a wedding or a funeral, and the odd first communion."

"This is where the river rose in about..." The pilgrims turned to look at him. "Let's have a wander up here."

In the shade of the trees he told us that according to the old man in 1089 a shepherd was trying to get his flock across the swollen stream when he saw an image of the Virgin either floating in the water or up against some rocks.

"Which was it?" I said.

"That's just what I asked the chap, and he said it didn't matter, so I asked him if the image was of stone or wood or something else, and he said that didn't matter either, but that about three hundred years later they built the sanctuary in honour of this supposed Virgin Mary."

I sighed. "And then you told him you thought it was a load of bollocks, I suppose."

"Er, not in so many words, but I did express a certain scepticism."

"That's when he was shaking his head," Diego said to me.

"Anyway, then he started going on about faith and that if what the shepherd saw was just a vision it didn't really matter. He said that the main benefit of revelations and relics and whatnot is to enable the faithful to concentrate their minds on our saviour."

"That's when he started looking thoughtful," I said to Diego.

"No, that was after he'd told me about his trip to Lourdes a couple of years ago. He had a really bad stomach and feared it might be cancer, but before going to the doctor's he nipped over the Pyrenees to Lourdes and had a good pray. When he got home the pain soon went away. What do you think of that?"

"Indigestion?" I said.

"No, he'd been poorly for weeks. Anyway, he then said that what mattered wasn't if the girl really saw the Virgin Mary in the cave near Lourdes in eighteen-fifty-something, but that she *believed* she did. She believed it, and so do the millions of pilgrims who go to Lourdes every year."

"Millions?" I said.

Diego nodded. "Yes, it's incredible there. I went when I was little and there were hundreds of people in wheelchairs all over the place. Some of them looked half-dead, but they do say that some people get cured there."

"That's just the law of averages," I said.

Frank raised a forefinger. "Or is it? That's the kind of thing a good documentary maker tries to find out."

"Uh-oh," I said.

"Yes, tomorrow I mean to come with my camera and set up shop near the grotto. I'll ask anyone who doesn't look like an idle tourist if they've had any experience of... well, miracles and things."

"And then upset them," said Diego.

"No, not at all. Maximum respect at all times. It's my job to be impartial and allow the viewers to decide if it's a lot of rot or not."

I chuckled and nudged Diego. "He's changed his tune."

"He'll still put his foot in it, you'll see."

"No, I won't," I said. "I'll just hear about it later. I'm going for a good long walk tomorrow."

"I'll join you."

Frank tipped back his head and sniffed. "I don't want you two hanging around anyway. I'm going to wear a shirt and trousers, so they'll take me seriously."

"Good for you. Come on, let's walk up the river and see if we spot any more virgins," I said.

Frank shook his head. "Oh, ye of little faith."

After another dip in the pool at about seven it was cool enough to set up our tiny stove and prepare an early dinner of pasta with tinned Bolognese sauce. Ours was a humble meal compared to those of the other campers, most of whom had multi-hob stoves or even gas barbecues.

"What do we do now?" I said at half past nine after I'd washed up.

"Wait for night to fall and get ourselves off to *ohea*," Frank said. "That's bed in Basque. The sun rises at 6.37 tomorrow, so I'll set my alarm for six."

"No-one else looks like they're thinking about going to bed," I said. "In fact some of them are just starting dinner."

Diego pushed himself to his feet, as we were the only campers without chairs, not to mention the tables, awnings, windbreaks, lamps, radios and sundry appurtenances that most of the others had. "I don't know about you two, but I'm off to the bar."

"You're setting a bad precedent, Diego," said Frank. "We're here to be at one with nature. We should be gazing at the moon, not fluorescent lights."

I stood up and gazed around the bustling field. "This is like bloody Glastonbury. I'll try not to wake you when I get back, Frank."

He took a swig of water. "Don't be too late."

Both the bar and restaurant were crowded and incredibly noisy, so we took our decaf coffees and glasses of Patxaran – a typically Basque sloe berry and aniseed liqueur – to a table outside. I found the drink refreshing and not too strong, so we ordered another, then a third, but when Diego suggested one more for the road I said we ought to be getting back. He twisted my arm easily enough, however, but half an hour later when he drawled that he'd like a nightcap I demurred.

"That's enough for tonight, Diego. It's half eleven and things have quietened down now."

He belched lightly. "Aw, jus' one more, Justin."

"But why?"

"Because I don't wanna get in that nasty tent," he whimpered. "I've already seen some bugs in it. I need to get pissed before I go to bed, tonight at least."

"You are pissed. Come on, I'll check your tent for scorpions before you get in it."

I led my grumbling friend away, but was called back by the lifeguard, now a waiter, who said it was customary to pay for what one consumed.

"Perdona," I said as I coughed up.

"I will watch you three," the uppity youth said in English. "You English drink too much."

I pointed at my shambling pal. "He's Spanish. He's a bad influence on us. Buenas noches."

He grunted goodnight.

After strapping on our only head torch I checked Diego's tent for creepy-crawlies and soon gave him the all-clear.

"Say a prayer to the Virgin if you feel nervous."

"I might. Goodnight."

I switched off the torch and crept into our tent, anxious not to wake Frank lest he start gabbing away. After climbing into my bag and zipping it up, as the night was quite cool, I luxuriated in the silence broken only by a few indistinct voices. When they ceased for a while I sensed that something was missing. Realising that it was Frank's breathing, I flicked on the torch and saw his empty sleeping bag. I pushed in a new pair of earplugs and soon fell asleep.

7

When I awoke at a quarter past eight Frank's sleeping bag was still empty. I didn't exactly panic, but on spotting rumpled underwear lying there I felt a mild sense of relief, as he must have come back, slept, and gone out again. On removing my earplugs I heard birdsong and subdued chatter, so I got dressed and emerged to find Diego facing the rising sun with a smile on his face and a canvas chair beneath him.

"Where did you get that?"

"Morning, Justin."

"Morning."

"Ah, it's going to be a lovely day. Did you sleep well?"

"Yes."

"Me too. My silly fear of camping has gone now."

"Great. We'll be able to take turns at sleeping alone then."

"Yes, well, give me a bit more time to get used to it."

"And the chair?"

He shrugged. "It was leaning on the car this morning. Frank must have borrowed it."

"Have you seen him? He wasn't here last night."

"No, and I've been up for half an hour. We could call him."

"Oh, I don't think so."

After a peaceful breakfast of instant coffee and pastries, we made a couple of sandwiches, bought water from the shop, and headed off along a trail to the west. We had no map, but by using satellite images on Diego's phone we managed to find our way through the woods to a pretty hamlet called Bellojín, where we had a drink in a typically Basque bar where no-one was speaking Basque. We got back to the campsite at about two and after a quick swim decided to avail ourselves of the fixed-price daily lunch in the restaurant. We'd hardly mentioned Frank all morning, having agreed to enjoy our time alone rather than spend it speculating on what he might have been up to since we last saw him.

As our inevitable reunion drew nearer, however, we began to hypothesise. I suggested that all the stream water he'd drunk had probably made him ill and that some kindly soul who'd seen him staggering back from the loo had lent him the chair to sit on until he had to go again. Diego thought that rather than capitulating and coming to the bar, he'd wandered around the field and got chatting to someone. We agreed that his early start was simply an attempt to impress us, and as he'd taken his camera and tripod we assumed he was still interviewing pilgrims by the grotto.

After coffee we strolled straight up there but didn't find him, so we called in at the bar to enquire.

"The foreigner with the camera?" said the man behind the counter. "I believe some priests drove him away."

Diego smiled. "Do you know why?"

He shrugged. "I heard talk that he upset another foreigner, and the priests thought he was spoiling the sanctity of the grotto, so they asked him to leave. I believe he refused to go, so they threatened to call the civil guard and then he went. Isn't he a friend of yours?"

"Just an acquaintance," Diego said, before filling me in on their rapid exchange.

"Oh, dear. So he did put his foot in it, after all. Let's go and see what he has to say for himself."

Frank was fast asleep on his mat, so we zipped up the tent to make sure he didn't catch a chill. He emerged a while later, pouring with sweat.

"Why did you shut it, you rotten buggers?"

"You told us we shouldn't have siestas. How did it go at the grotto?"

"Fine. I did a couple of good interviews."

"And where were you last night?"

"Chatting to some folk from Valencia at those tents over there. They lent me the chair you're sitting on, as they'd seen us lounging about like paupers. Pass me that bottle of water, please."

"Where's your stream water?"

"Oh, I drank it all."

Diego jumped up and grasped an empty bottle. "I'll get you some more."

"No, don't bother." He drank some mineral water. "I'm off for a swim."

By making no further enquiries we ensured that Frank told us the whole story little by little. By the time we set off to the village at eight we'd discovered that both of our hypotheses were right. The night before, not feeling at all sleepy, he'd strolled past a few tents and got chatting to two young couples who'd invited him to a mug of hot chocolate. This had caused some kind of chemical reaction in his stomach which had made him hotfoot it to the loo, after which the ladies had pampered him a bit and lent him the chair. He'd finally felt able to go to bed at two, before rushing to the toilet again when his alarm went off at six.

Not being the type of guy to let a spot of diarrhoea – caused by the hot chocolate, he insisted – hold him back, he'd drunk a chamomile tea and eaten some toast with olive oil in the bar, before making his way to the grotto. There he had, and I quote, frozen his balls off until the sun had risen above the hills and the first pilgrims had arrived to peruse the statue. One lady had asked him to move his camera away as she was trying to pray, so he'd retreated a few yards and soon found his first willing interviewee, a devout young man from Bilbao. His take on apparitions was similarly liberal to that of the old man from the day before, so they'd parted on good terms, and no sooner had Frank reviewed the footage than a lady from León had sidled up and soon found herself with a mic pinned to her jacket.

Her interpretation of Christianity was a little more rigid and they'd had a lively debate about the loaves and fishes, the provenance of all the bits of the True Cross in churches throughout the world, and other hot religious topics. Only when Frank expressed his doubts about the Resurrection did she started to get annoyed, but like all experienced spiritual documentary makers, he'd known how to diffuse the situation and wind up their exchange in a civilised way.

When we sat down to dinner in the village bar along with many other campers, only the bit about his run-in with the foreigner and the priests remained to be told.

"I'd just got back after having another chamomile in the bar when this party of Germans arrived. I know a bit of German, so I said *guten Morgen* and we got chatting."

"In German?" I asked.

"No, in English. They were Catholics from Bavaria who were visiting a few miraculous sites on their way to Santiago de Compostela, which is a real draw because some relics of Saint James's are supposed to be kept there. The stupid woman who I interviewed lost her rag because of them, in fact. Yes, she didn't mind me doubting apparitions of the Virgin, but when I touched on her bones she was furious."

"You touched her bones?" said Diego.

"Not hers, Saint James's. It so happens that last night while that damn hot chocolate was doing its worst I did a bit of research on my phone, and there's no *way* those bones are his. I mean, according to the bible he came to Spain, right, but then he went back home and got his head chopped off by the King of Judea. She agreed about that, but when I said that someone hauling his bones all the way back here was a bit far-fetched, she started fuming."

I chuckled. "Shouldn't you have used your spiritual documentary maker's diplomatic skills to calm her down?"

He sipped his mineral water and shook his head. "I tried. I said, look, there probably weren't all that many decent roads back then, as the Roman's hadn't been in charge for that long, let alone cheap flights." He sighed. "The bit about the cheap flights just slipped out. She started hollering at me and that's when the shirty priests came along. She gabbled something in crap Spanish about me being a provocative atheist and one of them grabbed my camera because I was still filming, or I thought I was, but the bloody battery had gone flat, damn it, so I've only got the nice interviews and the first bit of hers."

"The chap in the bar said you refused to go," I said.

"Too right. No-one grabs my camera, not even a man of God. It's my livelihood, or will be one day. No, I just stood my ground a bit to show them the sort of guy they were dealing with, then I strolled back. How was your walk?"

"Fine. We're thinking of heading off in the other direction tomorrow."

"Oh, the countryside around here's no great shakes, is it? Why don't we drive up to the coast?"

"Whereabouts?" Diego said.

He smiled. "How about Ondarroa?"

"Did you speak to your friend Karlos?"

"Hmm, my mum sent me his number. I rang it and got no reply, so I sent him a text saying I was nearby. It sounds like a pretty good place anyway. Not too touristy, but there's a campsite which hopefully won't be Butlin's under canvas like the one here. It'll be nice to swim in the sea too, instead of that busy pool that the kids piss in."

Diego winced.

"What do you reckon?" I asked him. "We said we might go to Ondarroa if he behaved here, but he hasn't really done that, has he?"

"Not really."

"Aw, but I want to go to a real Basque place where they speak Euskera."

Diego smiled. "Real Basques aren't like Catholic German ladies, you know. They're tough and proud, so if you put your foot in it, they might clubber you."

"Clobber you," I said.

"Clobber you. Thanks."

"You didn't see the German woman. She must be descended from the Hunnish hordes. I've learnt my lesson though. No more wisecracks from now on. How about it then?"

"We'll sleep on it," I said.

Frank got his way, of course, because the seaside was exerting a strong pull on us all, and Ondarroa seemed as good a place as any to begin our westbound coastal route. We waited until the tents were dry before striking camp and setting off at ten. Diego had strict instructions not to rush, and as we headed north-east along the motorway his speed rarely exceeded 130kph. On approaching Vitoria none of us felt inclined to visit the city, so we whizzed around it and soon entered a terrain of higher and even greener hills.

"Ah, we're in the Basque heartland now," said Frank. "*Astiro hitz egin mesedez*. You'd better learn how to say that."

"What does it mean?" I said from the back.

"Please speak more slowly."

Diego laughed. "What's the point of saying that if we don't know any Basque?"

"Speak for yourself. Hmm, I see your point though." He glanced at his phone. "Right, how about *Ba al dakizu ingelesez?* Do you speak English?"

Diego chuckled. "What for?"

"Well, I think they'd rather speak English than the language of the oppressor."

"What rubbish."

"Er, I hope this Karlos isn't some mad Basque fanatic," I said.

"No, he's a level-headed guy. He went into exile in Seville to improve his job prospects. He said that most folk in Ondarroa rarely leave Euskadi at all." He glanced down. "*Non dago komuna*. That's a useful one."

"Is that, no common dagos?" I said.

"No, where's the bathroom." He patted the camera battery that was recharging. "I wonder who I'll find to interview up there. I think I need a new angle. I've done enough religion for the time being, and I don't want to discuss politics, as that's just too obvious, although I suppose I could ask them about the time they kidnapped Revilla, seeing as he's a friend of mine."

"They didn't kidnap him, ETA did," said Diego. "You've got me worried now, Frank. If you're going to remind them of those days, me and Justin will wait for you in Cantabria. You can catch a bus or something."

"No, you're right, I mustn't utter a word about stuff like that. No doubt a new angle will occur to me when we get there."

On approaching the coast we left the motorway, joined a pleasant winding road, and caught our first glimpse of the Bay of Biscay before descending into Mutriku, a picturesque little town in a cove.

"We can walk here from the campsite," Diego said as he drove through. "It's between here and Ondarroa, so we'll be able to walk there too."

The narrow lane to the campsite meandered through stunning scenery and we agreed that we'd made a good choice. Diego soon pulled up outside reception.

"113km in an hour and a half. 4.6 litres per hundred kilometres. That's good."

Frank said *egun on* (good morning) to the lad behind the desk and was thrilled when he replied in Basque, before switching to the language of the oppressor and showing us to two small, shadeless pitches among several other tents.

"They've given the best pitches under the trees to the bloody motorhomes," Frank said as we unloaded the car. "I mean, they've got roofs to protect them from the sun."

"At least it's smaller and cheaper and there's no pool, so there might not be so many kids around," I said.

"Did you see those woods between here and the sea? We could have camped there for free. We'd just need plenty of water and a trowel to bury our shit. We'll have to try wild camping sometime."

"Count me out," said Diego. "I'm still getting used to normal camping." He looked at his phone. "We can walk to the beach, then on to the town to get some shopping."

After a ten-minute stroll down the hillside we reached a small, sandy beach opposite the harbour. Unfortunately Frank had caught a glimpse of another tiny beach to the right of a rocky outcrop.

"Ha, I've got my new angle," he said as we stripped off.

Diego sighed. "What is it?"

"That little nudist beach, of course. Did you not see all those bronzed buttocks?"

"Yes, and I hoped you hadn't." I smiled. "You can forget it anyway. The minute you appear with you camera and tripod they'll be up in arms. They'll drive you away like those priests did."

He chuckled. "I'm not so dense, Justin. No, I'll wander over there tomorrow with my camera in my bag. I'll get chatting to some friendly nudist and ask him, or preferably her, if I can film them from the waist up while they tell me what makes them want to sunbathe bollock-naked. Then we'll find a spot near the rocks where no-one else will be in the picture, though of course I'll do the odd swift panning shot on the sly. Yes, I think that'll work."

"You'll be naked yourself, of course," said Diego.

"Naturally on a naturist beach I'll be naked too. That goes without saying."

As we headed towards the water I told him he ought to go there right away to get a feel for it.

"You know, I think I will. I can do some groundwork and maybe line something up for tomorrow. Yes, a documentary maker must be prepared to go the extra mile to get what he wants. I feel like I've found my true vocation at last."

"Off you go then."

"Yes, well, right, yes…"

Diego clucked like a chicken, upon which Frank trotted back up the beach.

"Oh, the water's cold," Diego said when it lapped over our feet.

I clucked, so he raced into the low waves and I followed him. We managed a ten-minute swim before jogging back to our towels. We'd been sunbathing for a while when Frank appeared, still wet from the sea.

"Did you get your kit off?" I asked.

"Of course. Look, my shorts are dry."

"How was it?" Diego asked.

"Oh, the most natural thing in the world. Of course, like any red-blooded male I was a bit anxious about how I'd respond to all that female flesh, but it didn't even stir." He sat down on his towel. "Yes, I let it all hang out and no-one seemed to give me a second glance."

"Why would they?" I said.

"Well, I'm not badly endowed, you know, although the cold water did level the playing field a bit."

"So you've been walking around looking at your dick," I said. "That's great, Frank."

"No, I wasn't. Anyway, I got chatting to an oldish chap. He's been coming every summer for years. He was circumcised, so maybe he's Jewish or something."

I groaned. "So you've been looking at other people's dicks. That's even better."

"A quick glance. At first I thought he just had the skin pulled back, then I noticed it was all tight."

"Some glance," said Diego.

"I think you'd better skip these interviews, Frank. I've got a gut feeling that it's going to get you into trouble."

"Nonsense. The trouble is that I haven't really got a proper angle yet. I don't want to ask the usual trite questions about nudism. I need to come up with something more... more incisive." He took his phone from his bag. "Ooh, a message from Karlos. Let's see. He says he'll be back home for the weekend and to give him a call. What day is it?"

"Thursday."

"Hmm, maybe he'll invite us to stay at his house, or his parents' house."

I thought quickly. "Arrange to meet him tomorrow evening. Let him decide if he wants to invite us."

"Fair enough." He stretched the waistband of his swim shorts. "God, I find these restricting now."

"You know where to go to take them off," said Diego.

We ate lunch at a restaurant near the harbour, figuring that the midday menus were the best way to get most of our nutrients fairly cheaply, as our campsite dinners were always going to be rudimentary, unless we bought a decent stove and more pans. Ondarroa is more built up than Mutriku, but the red-roofed blocks of flats didn't seem out of place and made the best use of the small amount of flattish land on either side of the river. Many people were speaking Euskera and a leathery old man seemed genuinely pleased when Frank told him in his own tongue that his town was very pleasant, having first listened to the phrase several times on his smartphone.

"The Basque Country is definitely different," he said as we tucked into our *marmitako*, a tasty tuna stew.

"The people seem friendly," I said.

"More friendly than people from my town?" said Diego.

"Er, no, about the same. I'm only going on my first impressions, of course."

He smiled. "I sometimes think that us Olvegueños are like the Basques in some ways. We're also industrious and independent."

"So are other Sorianos lazy and dependent?" Frank asked.

"Well, no, they're all good, hard-working people, but they don't have the opportunities that we have."

Frank smiled at me. "For every Spaniard their town or village is the best in the world. Anyway, it's crossed my mind that it'd be brilliant to come and live in the Basque Country. Wouldn't it be great to learn a language that hardly anyone else knows?"

"Don't look at me. I can't even speak Spanish."

"You know, your best bet would be to skip Spanish and concentrate on your Euskera. Ha, you'd become a totally unique person, probably."

"Yes, Frank."

"And as Euskera's nothing like any other language, it'd be a real challenge for us, especially at our age."

I nodded and sipped my Txakoli, the light, lightly sparkling white wine which Frank had recommended. Although the idea of moving to Spain appealed to me more with each passing day, living somewhere with Frank didn't. I wouldn't mind having him nearby, say ten or fifteen miles away, but to share a house or even a village with him would be a recipe for... well, maybe not disaster, but certainly dependence. Neither he nor Diego had made much effort to speak to me in Spanish and if I lived cheek by jowl with either of them I'd have an interpreter on hand most of the time. No, if I ever moved to Spain I'd have to go it alone, so Frank's use of 'we' was a little worrying, as although I'm apt to mock him in these pages, I knew I oughtn't to underestimate his considerable powers of persuasion.

"Spanish would be quite enough of a challenge for me, Frank," I said, preparing to nip any cohabitation plans in the bud.

"Yes, I guess I'm just keen on Euskadi because we're here. No doubt when I get to Cantabria and Asturias I'll feel the same way about those green and pleasant lands. Houses aren't that cheap to rent here anyway. I've already had a look. We'll just have to keep our eyes and minds open, eh?"

A good anti-pestering tactic occurred to me. "I won't be going anywhere for at least a couple of years. I'm not one to rush into things, so I'll get another job and maybe come back again to visit next summer." I sipped and smiled.

He fiddled with his phone and frowned. "*Zentzugabekeria*. God, what a mouthful."

"I bet it means bollocks," said Diego.

"Sort of. It means nonsense. Nonsense, Justin. Before this trip's over you'll have realised that Blackburn is no place to be. Spain will have seduced you, you'll see."

He then changed the subject, but I warned myself to be on my guard, or before I knew it I'd be signing a rental contract for a house in some one-horse hamlet with only Frank and a few oldies and goats for company. That's how well I knew my oldest and most infuriating friend.

8

Despite the proximity of the other tents we had a pleasant evening and got a good night's sleep. The next day dawned bright and Karlos was due at the campsite at 8pm, so we just had to ensure that Frank got through the day without being arrested or beaten to a pulp by a horde of furious nudists.

"I'm going to use the in-camera mic for once," he said as he packed his knapsack. "It isn't brilliant, but I can't really clip one on their nipples, can I?" He pushed back his scanty hair and sighed. "I had a brilliant idea earlier, then realised that neither of you would be man enough to cooperate."

I kept my mouth shut and nodded, but Diego asked him what it was.

"Well, I thought you could come to the nudist beach too, but pretend you didn't know me. I could saunter over and we'd get chatting, then we'd do a short interview by the rocks. That might encourage someone else to do one too. You'd have broken the ice, you see."

"Count me out," I said. "I don't fancy stripping off at all."

"I'll do it," said Diego, then to me. "That way I'll be able to keep an eye on him. At the first sign of trouble I'll drag him off the beach by his... hair."

Frank smiled. "Thanks, Diego. I assure you there won't be any trouble, but it's good to know that one can count on at least one of one's friends. Ah, old friends are all very well, but newer friends are often truer and more understanding. Old friends are like a habit that's hard to break, like... like an old jacket that you hate to discard, whereas newer friends, like newer jackets, actually suit you much bet–"

"Save your breath," I snapped. "I'm still not coming."

"Oh, come on, Justin," said Diego, taken in by Frank's blathering. "It'll be a new experience for both of us."

"Don't rush him, Diego. He needs a little time to get his head around the idea. You two go to the normal beach first, then when you come over to the Garden of Eden, or Beach of Eden, he might pluck up the courage to follow in your enlightened footsteps."

To shut him up I told him I'd think it over and we soon made our way down to our respective beaches. Diego tried to persuade me to cross the clothing barrier, and after refusing again I said I might keep an eye on them from the rocks, just to show a little solidarity.

"Suit yourself," he said, before stomping off in something approaching a huff. After a while I thought I'd better do as I'd promised, so I packed up my stuff, put on my sandals and scaled the spur between the beaches. On reaching the top I found some small trees among which to conceal myself, so I settled down to await developments. My friends were already chatting amiably and when Frank took out his camera Diego began to quiz him about it. They then stood up, approached the rocks to the seaward side of where I was hiding, and without more ado Frank began to interview him. I surveyed the nearby nudists for signs of disquiet or annoyance, but only a few eyed them with mild curiosity. On concluding their five-minute farce, Frank and Diego shook hands and headed back to their towels, but Frank stopped beside a middle-aged couple who had asked him something. He was clearly giving them some sort of spiel and the bronzed, buxom lady soon got to her feet and followed him over to the rocks.

At this point I became a little nervous, because her husband, a huge bull of a man who might well have been a fortieth-generation Basque, approached and stood beside Frank as he raised the camera and indicated that filming had begun. With his beefy arms folded and a smile playing on his craggy face, he resembled a nightclub bouncer ready to eject any undesirables. I feared that when (not if) Frank forgot himself and said something stupid, the man would wrest the precious camera from his grasp and smash it on the rocks, but I needn't have worried, or not about that, because after a few minutes of lively conversation the man spotted me among the foliage.

His hands fell and he clenched his mighty fists, before emitting a tremendous roar and yelling in Spanish, "Hey, what are you doing there?"

I ducked.

"Yes, you, you bloody pervert! Grrr, just wait till I get my hands on you!" he bellowed, before making for the rocks like an enraged ape, him being a hirsute sort of chap.

Sensing that an explanation of my mission would fall on deaf ears, I grabbed my bag, scampered through the trees, and slid down the rocks, before jogging along the beach with apparent insouciance, I hoped. Had he been a younger man he might have nabbed me, but I knew I had at least a minute's head start, so on reaching the car park at the end I slowed to a walk and looked over my shoulder. There he was, stomping along with one hand in the air and the other maintaining his modesty, so I trotted onto the road, sure that he wouldn't dare to continue his pursuit, if only because he was barefoot. On reaching the town I entered a small tavern well away from the harbour, where I ordered a beer and waited for my phone to ring. I was sure that Frank would lose no time in chastising me for ruining his interview, but after a second beer he hadn't called, so I made my way back to the campsite along the road, having seen enough of the beach for one day.

I could have called them to see if the coast was clear, of course, but instead I ate a can of spaghetti and some stale bread for lunch, before having a kip in the shade of the car. At about four o'clock Frank kicked my foot and when I saw his ugly mug beaming down at me I feared that the post-mortem would be a protracted one.

"We've just had an *excellent* lunch, Justin," he said.

"Ah, good."

"He insisted on paying."

"Who?"

"Andoni, of course. The chap who you so rudely ran away from."

I yawned. "It seemed prudent at the time. He chased me along the beach, you know."

"Ha, only to tell you to stop. I followed him up the rocks and told him you were my mate, but only he had the balls to run along the normal beach."

"I see."

"I interviewed him after his wife, then a while later he drove us into town and took us to their favourite restaurant. No fixed-price menu for us today, no siree." He patted his stomach. "I'd never eaten fresh lobster before. Yes, Andoni and Arantxa are from Basauri, near Bilbao, and they've got an apartment here."

"How did the interviews go?"

"Great. In fact the one with Andoni might well be among the most original interviews in the history of film-making. Don't you reckon, Diego?"

"It was unusual, yes. I've certainly never seen anything quite like it."

Frank kicked my other foot. "Get up and you can see for yourself. I'll just pop the other battery in."

The interview with Andoni wasn't remarkable in itself, in the sense that if you merely listened to it you'd hear a man talking about the small scrapyard that he'd inherited from his father and turned into a booming business, his twenty years of bull running – including one minor goring – at the San Fermín fiestas in Pamplona, his happy marriage to a like-minded spouse, their three children and two young grandchildren, his penchant for fresh seafood, and finally an invitation to lunch which Frank said he might have to cut before slotting the interview into his *The Changing Face of Spain* documentary. Pretty mundane stuff really, except that Frank filmed him from the knees up and not once did Andoni show any awareness of his nakedness. He gesticulated quite a lot and when his broad shoulders moved you couldn't help but see his willy sway from side to side like a fleshy pendulum. When it stopped I found myself waiting for him to set it off again, all the while half listening to his nonchalant chatter and the odd comment from Frank.

I was waiting for one more sway when the film ended. Having always considered myself to be wholly heterosexual, I asked Diego what had grabbed his attention the most.

"His dick, of course."

"Thank God for that."

"That and the fact that he was so chilled out, just chatting away without a care in the world."

I looked at Frank. "It was a curious thing to watch, but I don't quite see how it's among the most original interviews in the history of film-making."

"I challenge you to go online and find me a filmed interview of a nudist who doesn't even mention nudism. Why interview nudists? I'll tell you, because they're nudists. Always the same scratched record. 'Yes, I do this because I feel so free and blah blah blah.' 'Don't you feel that other people might not understand you because blah blah blah?' 'Yes, but it's our right as people to blah blah blah.'"

"I've got the idea, Frank. I have to admit that it's quite a coup in its way, but would Andoni mind if you showed it to the world?"

"Mind? He'd be delighted, I think."

"Right. Oh, what was the interview with his wife like?"

"Oh, that was all blah blah blah about bloody nudism, then a short interruption because some weirdo was spying on us, then more of the same. It was only from the waist up too. I probably won't even use it, as it'd lessen the impact of Andoni's superb little show."

"Well, I'm really glad it went so well," I said with an ingratiating grin.

He frowned. "And as for your little performance, the less said the better."

"That suits me, Frank. Will you been seeing them again?"

"No, they're off home. That beach gets too busy at the weekends."

I recalled the hulking Basque bounding along the other beach. "That's a shame."

Karlos proved to be a slim, softly spoken chap in his thirties who seemed really pleased that Frank had given up the booze. Over dinner in the campsite restaurant he told us about their nocturnal adventures in Seville, where Frank took him to many dives in Triana, one of the oldest and certainly the most authentic neighbourhood of the city. There they drank cheap wine and watched impromptu flamenco performances until the early hours.

"I always had to make him go home," Karlos said in Spanish. "He would have stayed all night, drinking and talking to the folk.

We had some good times there, but I'm glad you've given up alcohol, Frank. I could see it was taking hold of you. How did you get on in Almería? I expected to hear from you, but you never called or replied to my texts."

"Oh, I went from bad to worse there, and I didn't have a friend like you to keep me under control." He told him how his desperate prayer was eventually answered back home in Blackburn, partly thanks to me.

Karlos smiled. "I never expected you to go home. You always told me how you hated England and would never go back, but I suppose the inheritance was a key factor."

"Yes, and I was about to lose my job anyway. I'd already been warned about coming to work looking like a tramp and stinking of booze. It was truly providential."

Karlos sipped his beer. "And don't you mind other people drinking?"

"Not at all. I don't think I'd like to be with people getting drunk, but these two are just social drinkers. And how about you, Karlos? How have you been getting on?"

Karlos's time in Seville had paid off and he'd got a better position based in Donostia, aka San Sebastian, although he travelled around a lot, supervising internet cable repairs and suchlike. He was due to marry his fiancée Nerea in the autumn and they were busy furnishing their new flat in Ondarroa.

"Er... *zorionak*, Karlos," Frank said, before shaking his hand.

"Gracias, Frank, or *eskerrik asko*. I see you still remember some of the Euskera I taught you."

He nodded. "*Bai*, and I've learnt a bit more. Justin and I are thinking of renting a house in Euskadi, or maybe in Cantabria or Asturias."

Due to his recent good behaviour and the fact that he'd let me off the hook regarding my humiliating escape from the apparently raging Andoni, I didn't bother contradicting his bold assertion. Besides, I was keen to know what a native Basque thought about Frank's idea.

"Is Euskera really hard to learn?" I asked Karlos.

He chuckled. "It wasn't for me, but yes, I believe it's one of the most difficult languages, due to its complex grammar. There are also many different dialects, so the Euskera you hear on television isn't the same as that spoken in each area. To be honest, if I were you I'd choose another place to live where they speak only Spanish."

"But Justin and I are up for a challenge, Karlos. Aren't we, Justin?"

I smiled.

"Hmm, but Euskera might be too much of a challenge. Frank, you'll be old before you learn it, if you ever do, and you speak fluent Spanish anyway. Justin, you already know some Spanish and you'll soon be able to speak it well. Here you'd seem much more like outsiders, I'm afraid."

"Ah, but in Cantabria and Asturias they have their own dialects too," said Frank.

"Oh, they're much easier to learn. They're just variations of Spanish, but don't tell an Asturian that. Catalan too is quite easy, for the same reason."

"How come it's the Catalans who're now crying out for independence, while the Basques don't seem to be doing much about it?" Frank said.

"Oh, no politics, please," said Diego.

Karlos shrugged. "I think a lot of us are fed up of the whole independence business and satisfied with what we have. We're autonomous, we have our own parliament, and most of our representatives in the Spanish parliament belong to Basque parties. What more do we want?"

"But would you personally like to see an independent Euskadi?" Frank asked him.

"Not especially. I suppose it's a nice idea, but I don't feel any less Basque by being Spanish too. Besides, now is no time for us to divide into smaller countries. The problems of today's world must be faced with unity, not division."

"I agree," I said, having voted to remain in the Brexit referendum. Frank would have too, but he'd been too busy getting drunk to sort out his postal vote.

Diego asked Karlos if the commute to Donostia wasn't rather a long one.

"Just an hour if I set off early. Nerea and I prefer to live here to be close to our families."

Frank cleared his throat. "Karlos, do you remember a chap called Emiliano Revilla?"

Diego and I groaned.

"The name rings a bell. Who is he?"

"A friend of mine, since an interview we had a few days ago. He's an old man now, but ETA kidnapped him back in 1988."

Karlos shrugged. "One of many, I'm afraid." His yawn was sudden and unconvincing. "Well, I'll have to be going now. I was up at six this morning."

"Have a coffee," said Frank. "Sorry I mentioned that, but I just remembered him. Our interview was quite interesting."

Diego snorted. "That's one word for it."

Frank told the tale in a humorous way and we all laughed when he re-enacted Señor Revilla's eruption.

"I'm not surprised, poor man," said Karlos. "We all want to forget about those times, especially the older folk who lived through them. Under Franco we felt the need to fight back after so many years of oppression, but after he died there was no excuse for more violence. ETA was like a mafia. They extorted money from everyone who had any, including hundreds of Basques. Even many of the radicals who supported them know deep down that they were wrong. Now I'd prefer to change the subject."

"Fair enough," said Frank, before telling him about his other pioneering interviews.

"Yes, Frank, I think you'd certainly be better off finding somewhere to live outside Euskadi," Karlos said when he'd stopped laughing. "Being the way you are, with or without alcohol, you'd soon put your foot in it and upset people. Although we're not in the news so much nowadays, feelings still run high in certain quarters." He patted his hand. "If you and Justin do end up living in the north you must come to visit me and my wife. You too, Diego."

Frank smiled. "We'll definitely do that, won't we, Justin?"

"Sí, Frank."

Karlos yawned. "Now I really must go. I'm exhausted. I'm busy this weekend, but we must stay in touch and I'm sure we'll see each other again soon."

We stood up and shook hands.

"*Laster arte*," said Karlos. "That means see you soon."

"I knew that," said Frank. "*Laster arte*, Karlos."

Diego and I said it too and he left.

"Nice guy," said Diego.

"Very level-headed," I said.

Frank frowned. "Hmm, I thought I might get an invite to his wedding."

"Maybe you would have if you hadn't mentioned ETA," said Diego. "I know for a fact that not all Basques are as liberal as him. He'd be worried about what you might say at the reception, especially after what you told him about your recent interviews."

"I'd have liked to have met his bird too. We were quite close in Seville, but I suppose we did lose touch. I'll tell you what though; what he said about Euskera makes me even keener to learn it. It can't be all that hard. I mean, it's not as if they have different writing like Arabic and Chinese and whatnot."

I had an amusing thought and made the mistake of articulating it. "Hey, Frank, you could live in Euskadi and I could find a place in Cantabria or somewhere. Then we'd be close, but not too close."

His eyes sparkled and his hand came down upon mine. "Do you see what I mean now, Justin? The longer you're here, the more dreadful Blackburn's going to seem." He squeezed my hand. "I perceive a lot of sincerity in your little jest."

"Er, it wasn't a jest, Frank. If I did move here, I'd rather live on my ow–"

"Ha, Diego, it looks like you aren't going to get your way after all, eh?"

"What was my way, Frank?"

"Making us work for another ten years, you rotten sod."

He shrugged and raised his hands. "That's just my opinion. You're both free to do as you wish with your lives, but bear one thing in mind. If you go down that route of… well, of being poor, you'll struggle to find a decent woman who'll have you, either of you."

"Bah, a discerning woman sees beyond material things."

"I'm not so sure about that," I said. "I just remembered something I learnt when I was reading about Buddhism a few years ago. It's called the Middle Way. I didn't really buy all the stuff about reincarnation, but the Middle Way makes a lot of sense."

"And what, pray, is the middle way?" said Frank.

"Just what it says. For the monks it means not indulging in too much pleasure, but not going over the top with the self-mortification either. In our case it means not working our balls off for at least ten more years, but not living like paupers either."

"But I–"

It was my turn to interrupt. "For me that means finding a way to make a steady income. It doesn't have to be all that much, but enough to cover my costs."

"But that's what I've been saying all along."

"*Without* touching my savings."

"Hmm."

"This middle way sounds better than Frank's silly way," said Diego. "Frank thinks he'll make a bit of money here and there, but that won't be enough. One bad year and a few thousand have gone. Before you know it you'll no longer have a lot of savings. You must have a steady income. Please think about that before you do anything rash. Now, do you want to stay here this weekend, or move on to our next destination?"

"I'm easy," I said.

"At our next destination we're staying at a cheap but comfortable hotel."

"Oh, I think we've just about done Ondarroa now, don't you?" said Frank.

I could almost feel the clean sheets and the mattress beneath me. "Yes, I think so."

Diego grinned. "That's settled then. I'll book it right away."

Back at the tent I was already kneading my earplugs into shape when Frank revived the subject of earning a living in Spain. Having suddenly decided that teaching English was a doddle, he said that in a biggish village we could probably both get quite a few private classes. Not wishing to start a midnight debate, I agreed that English classes might be an option for us, but after saying goodnight and inserting my plugs I began to ponder on the possibilities of my own profession. Nowadays almost all accounting and bookkeeping tasks are done on the computer, of course, and although a self-employed bookkeeper tends to visit his customers quite often, surely there was work to be had which didn't necessitate paying any visits at all. These days more and more people are working remotely, so I resolved to do some research. I'd probably need to splash out on expensive software, and a good internet connection would be essential, but with those two factors covered, plus some customers, I could live anywhere I wished. Eager to share this minor epiphany, I eased out an earplug, but Frank was already snoring.

9

After sleeping on it I decided to keep this means of earning my bread from Frank for the time being, lest he start making joint plans right away. I knew that after exploring the coast we were due to visit Astorga in León, and after that we might well continue south to see Diego's errant uncle in Fermoselle, before heading back towards Soria. I intended to peruse each place along the way and commit myself to nothing. Once we were back in Ólvega I could coolly appraise the journey and maybe make some arrangements before heading home. That was the plan anyway, and as we sped west along the motorway I thought I might even stick to it.

"113 kilometres in one and a quarter hours. 4.7 litres per hundred kilometres," Diego said after pulling up outside a shabby *pensión* in Castro Urdiales, the easternmost seaside town in Cantabria. We climbed out and stretched our legs.

"This is quite a metropolis, Diego," Frank said. "Not exactly the quaint fishing village I envisaged."

"In the more popular resorts further west the hotels are either expensive or fully booked. I found a really good deal for us here."

"Yes, in a place over a shop, overlooking those lovely blocks of flats, and a long way from the beach."

"Only two minutes' walk, according to the info."

"What's this place got to offer, Diego, apart from petrol fumes?" I asked.

He looked at his phone. "Er, lovely beaches, a spectacular coastline with lots of cliffs, a fishing port, the old town, a castle, a nice park, and a lovely promenade, according to this."

"That sounds good," I said.

Frank looked up at the cracked plastic sign. "I'm not convinced. It isn't too late to move on to somewhere else."

"And it's going to cost us €52 a night."

"Each?" I squeaked.

"No, altogether, for a triple room. Pretty cheap, eh?"

"Well, it'll certainly do for one night," said Frank.

"Yes, well, to get that price I had to book us in for four nights. Just for the weekend would have been much dearer. It is July, you know."

Frank frowned. "Diego, although we're grateful for the research you've done, I'm afraid you've exceeded your executive powers. You should have consulted us first before making such a rash decision. I mean, look at all those bloody flats."

"Oh, I needed a rest from camping. Sleeping on a crappy mat, the insects, hairs in the showers, *pubic* hairs on the toilet seats."

"He has a point," said the conciliatory one.

"And we did say that we ought to stay in each place for some time."

Frank sighed. "All right, but be it on your head if we get bored to death. We may mutiny and appoint a new leader."

I gulped. "Diego's done a good job so far, on the whole."

The nice hard mattresses lessened Frank's indignation and when we allowed him to have the double bed he cheered up somewhat. The lack of an en suite bathroom was a minor blow, but by the time we'd seen some fine buildings on the seafront and reached a beach in a pleasant bay to the east of the busy harbour, the shabbiness of our lodgings no longer bothered us.

"It's just a place to kip, after all," said Frank as he sat on his towel applying sun cream. "Here we should buy our lunch at a supermarket and eat out in the evenings. Yes, it's going to be a nice break from camping, but I can't laze around the whole time. I'll take my camera out later and find someone to interview."

I chuckled. "Do you have an angle here yet, Frank?"

"No, I'll play it by ear. I didn't have an angle at the nudist beach and look how well it turned out."

"I thought the nudist beach *was* your angle," said Diego.

"Yes, well, I sought an angle within an angle."

"A very acute angle," I quipped.

"But in the end the sheer... mundanity of Andoni's chatter was what made it work so well." He shrugged. "I'm still learning really. I think it's more a question of sniffing out opportunities and getting stuck in than working out angles and whatnot."

Diego looked around the busy beach, then at the five and six-storey blocks behind us. "I bet there's plenty of demand for English classes here."

"I wouldn't like to live in such a big, touristy place," I said. "Maybe near it, but not in it."

"Yes, Justin, but we must begin to think about our work, now that we've resolved to follow this middle way of yours," said a now recumbent Frank.

"Buddha himself came up with it first, or so they say." I leapt up and trotted into the sea, out of harm's way.

Our first two days in Castro Urdiales were pleasant but unremarkable. We spent some time on the beach, visited the impressive church, toured the renovated castle with its more modern lighthouse, took snapshots of the purportedly Roman bridge, knocked around the streets of the old quarter and sat in the lovely main square, chilled out of an evening in the cafes near the harbour, and generally behaved like good, inquisitive, harmless tourists. Frank's video camera rarely left his knapsack and all was peace and harmony, until Monday lunchtime, when fate decreed that we skip our soggy supermarket sandwiches and enjoy a twelve-euro *menú del día* at a modest restaurant two streets back from the harbour.

The place was quite busy, the clientele comprising both workers and tourists, and we'd just tucked into our fish in green sauce when Frank began to goggle. I turned to glance at the object of his goggling and saw a pretty young woman with dark hair, almost black eyes, relatively pale skin, a round face, a cute little nose and full lips. Her expression was rather naive and innocent, and when she found us both looking at her, her mouth tightened and she lowered her eyes. Frank gazed at his plate and appeared to have lost control of his lower jaw.

"Don't you like it, Frank?" said Diego, oblivious to his goggling.

He shook his head. "The likeness is unbelievable. She's her spitting image."

"It's hake, Frank."

"I can just picture her leaning against that hideous wallpaper with her arms folded as she gazes at poor Umberto D. sitting on his narrow bed."

Diego rubbed his eyes.

"I think he's talking about that girl over there," I said. "The one with the older woman who might be her mum. Don't look again, Frank, or you'll frighten her."

"I don't need to look again. Her face is etched on my memory. Diego, you're nearest. Are they speaking Italian?"

He leant back and listened. "Nope, Spanish." He glanced around. "She's nothing special and she's far too young for you anyway."

Frank sighed. "I don't suppose either of you ignoramuses have even heard of Maria-Pia Casilio, have you?"

We hadn't.

"I'm not surprised really, because she wasn't that famous outside Italy," he said before filling us in on the then amateur actress's debut in Vittorio de Sica's 1952 film, *Umberto D.*, later to be considered a classic of world cinema, according to him. She'd gone on to make several more films, but would always be remembered for her role as the maid in that cinematic marvel.

"The thing is, Umberto D. was an old man who was about to lose his room in the lodging house where she worked. She tried to cheer him up, but it turned out she was pregnant and wasn't sure who the father was, so she was in just as big a fix as he was. That's what makes her performance so poignant really. Without her the film wouldn't be half as good." He stole a quick glance. "Diego, listen in and tell me what sort of voice she's got."

Diego leant back and had I not grasped his knee he might have heard her from floor-level.

"Well?"

"Quite pleasant, good pronunciation."

"Is it nasal at all?"

"Er, I'm not sure, Frank."

"Is it nasal at all?" he repeated in a nasal voice.

"No, I wouldn't say so."

"Damn, Maria-Pia's voice had a lovely nasal tone. If she hadn't had that voice I don't think the film would have gone down in history. Her voice gave it that special, ineffable something. Still, one can't have everything. Ha!" he cried, causing many heads to turn. He took out his phone. "I sometimes forget I've got this thing," he said as he swiped and jabbed. "Hmm, she's got make-up on in this one... yes, this one's from the film." He handed me the device. "Do you see what I mean now?"

I looked at the black and white photo, dropped my napkin in order to take another peek at the girl, then zoomed in on the face in the photo. "Yes, she is quite like her, but in colour, of course."

Diego looked at the screen. "Yes, she's very similar, but so what?"

"So what? You don't think I'm going to miss an opportunity like this, do you?"

Stereo groan.

"Justin, what course are they on?"

"Er, the main, I think."

"Good, that gives us time to think."

"I've already thought," I said. "I'm going to have coffee elsewhere."

"No, no, come on now. I'll need your help. I've somehow got to convince her that I'm not a weirdo or some sort of voyeur. We've got to come up with a good reason to film her."

"Film her doing what?" I said.

"Acting, of course." He placed his elbows on the table and rubbed his temples.

I nudged him. "Frank, if you just step outside before she does, you'll be able to film her from across the street as she leaves. Won't that do you?"

"Or just swap chairs and film her on your phone in here," said Diego. "She won't even know."

His head rose and there was fire in those big blue eyes. "Boys, you're about to make your movie debuts."

"Oh..."

"But..."

"Shush, and listen to my plan. All we have to do now is convince her to take part in a short film which we'll make tomorrow or whenever she's available. Diego, as you're Spanish you can be the producer too. I'm a well-known… no, an up-and-coming British film-maker who's here to film a… an anthological film, yes, like the great De Sica's *The Gold of Naples* or something. Oh, it's such a shame that she won't know who she is… but no, maybe it's better not to mention Maria-Pia at all, or not until later. So, Diego, when they're drinking coffee, can you slip over and put it to her?"

"Don't do…" I began, but had the sense not to proceed.

Diego sighed. "Justin, he's almost given Revilla a heart attack, he's been chased away by priests, and he's filmed two nudists. What harm can one more little film do? She'll probably say no anyway, but I'll do my best."

Frank slapped him on the back and gave me a swift glare. "Diego, you're a star. It's at times like these when one finds out who one's friend really–"

"Just a minute," I said. "You told me you'd left your scripts at home. If I recall rightly, you said you'd realised they were pretentious rubbish."

He flapped his hand. "Not a problem. Later on I'll knock something up for a divine young Spanish lady, a true Spanish gentleman, and a dozy foreigner who they cross paths with for some reason."

I glanced at Frank's quarry and her companion, just two women minding their own business. I calculated the odds of her being willing to take part in Frank's impromptu production and decided to take a risk, as it would prevent a lot of nagging and future recriminations.

"I'll do it as long as you don't make my part too daft," I said.

"Good lad." He turned to Diego. "It's all in your hands now. Once you've got talking you can give me the nod whenever you want and I'll come over."

Our desserts arrived.

"You'd better put your thinking cap on, Frank," I said. "She might want to know what the film's about, then there's the small matter of her learning her lines."

"Hmm, yes, and the location." he spooned half a flan into his mouth.

"How about near the castle?" Diego said.

"Hmm, too many people," he mumbled.

"That viewing place just past it might be best," I said.

"Yes, yes, we'll be able to shoo folk away from there and the sea should drown out other noises. Good thinking, Justin. Ha, I'm sure we'll make many a film together when we settle down somewhere."

Don't bet on it, I thought.

"Right, so that's the location. Diego, just tell her it's a little drama. We'll rehearse tomorrow and film on Wednesday. Their coffees have come. Off you go, and good luck."

I kept my fingers crossed under the table and when the older lady invited Diego to take a seat I tapped them against the leg, but judging by their smiles and nods the filming would be going ahead.

"I want a nice part without too many lines," I said to Frank.

"Yes, yes." He turned and fluttered his fingers at them, then Diego beckoned him over. I shifted my chair and watched him prattling away and when the waiter arrived I had their coffees sent over. Frank eventually remembered my existence and gave me the nod, so I took my chair and joined them.

"Fetch my bag, please, Justin, there's a good man," Frank said in English, and he was soon showing them his camera, just a small one he used when travelling between his major projects back home, he said. Catalina and Marta were indeed mother and daughter. They hailed from Valladolid and had a summer place in Castro Urdiales, where Catalina's husband joined them at the weekends until his holiday in August. They were pleasant and chatty and didn't seem to find it odd that some complete strangers wished to make a film with them, because Catalina had already hinted that she wouldn't mind having a bash, to which Frank had coolly replied that in one of the four short scripts which he intended to film in different parts of Spain he had just the part for her. Marta, who was twenty-two, suggested we make the film at a place a little way to the north of town where the sea formed a natural swimming pool among the rocks.

"There shouldn't be too many people around midweek," she said.

"We can rehearse this afternoon, if you like," said her mother, a slim lady of about fifty.

"Oh, I'll have to go and study the location first," said Frank. "How about if we meet at ten tomorrow?"

"What shall we wear?" Marta asked.

"Clothes like those. It's a contemporary film about… well, quotidian events."

"Oh, can you tell us about it?" said Marta's mum.

"It's better for you not to know yet. That way it'll be more spontaneous."

"But we could learn our lines before tomorrow. Wouldn't that make it easier?" said Marta.

The great charlatan remained unruffled. "Like the great Ingmar Bergman, I always prefer my actors to first study their parts on location. We can rehearse tomorrow and film the next day, if that's all right with you."

"Yes, we've nothing better to do," said Marta. "Do you have any of your films online, on YouTube or somewhere? I'd like to have a look."

"I'm afraid not. My... my last film will be appearing in the out-of-competition section at the Venice Film Festival this year, so I don't want anyone to get a preview."

"Ooh, when's that?"

Frank smiled. "In September."

"How exciting," said Catalina. "What's it about?"

He sipped his coffee, opened his mouth, then sipped again. "It's about an old man who's about to become homeless and a young lady who tries to help him. It's really a homage to the great Italian film *Umberto D*. Have you seen it?"

Neither of them had.

"Ha, the young actress in the film is quite similar to you in some ways, Marta. I think that's why I spotted you. Oh, and please don't wear any makeup tomorrow."

"I rarely wear any."

"What about me?" said Catalina.

"Not too much."

When the waiter arrived Frank insisted on paying their bill, explaining that he had a generous expense account, and we soon saw them out before returning to our table.

"Well, well, well," I said, feeling a bit stunned by this turn of events.

"Let this be a lesson to you, Justin."

"What? How?"

He settled into his preaching position. "In this life if one doesn't take a leap into the unknown from time to time, one achieves nothing, or next to nothing. They might well have fobbed me off, or rather Diego, but they didn't and now we have something exciting to look forward to. Who dares wins, Justin, as I'm sure I've said before."

"You haven't, but I'm sure you'll say it again."

He sighed. "Now I must repair to our humble lodgings and come up with something worthy of our new friends, especially young Marta. Ah, Marta, Maria; Maria, Marta. Who knows, maybe Marta will become the new Maria-Pia Casilio thanks to my... our efforts. While I'm toiling away you could do worse than watch a bit of *Umberto D*. I think there are some excerpts on YouTube."

"If Marta sees it she might think you're some sort of fetishist," I said.

"No, she'll just see her predecessor's genius and hopefully try to emulate her. Right, I'd better be off."

"Do you not want any help?" Diego said.

He shook his head weightily. "No, thanks, Diego. Your input might distract me from my aim."

"Which is?" I said.

"To make Marta shine, of course. Hmm, I think you and mother will be bit players, Justin."

"Suits me."

"Whereas Diego will have to step into shoes similar to those of the wonderful Carlos Battisti, who played Umberto D. and was, by the way, principally a linguist and only an occasional actor. Like the great Vittorio De Sica, I mean to use mostly amateur actors in my films."

"As if you had any choice," I said.

He grabbed his bag and stood up.

I prodded the bill. "You can pay this from you generous expense account."

"No, that's only for my stars. Ta ta, now." He swept out of the restaurant like an oversized Woody Allen, wisps of his unkempt hair fluttering as he opened the door, before he swept back in and hurried over.

"Er, you'd better go and have a look at this place where we're filming. I haven't got time. I'll call you in a bit. Bye." He left again.

Diego paid and we headed north to the Ostende Beach, beyond which lay our location. As we strolled along the promenade I asked Diego if he thought Frank's bullshit had been strictly necessary.

He chuckled. "He couldn't help himself. When he talks about films he enters a fantasy world. I think the interviews have just been a substitute for his true love."

"Yes, he was always knocked back in Blackburn, but Marta and her mum seem really keen. Do you think folk in Ólvega would be up for a bit of acting?"

"Hmm, possibly, the ones who aren't too busy. I hope he writes a good part for me. I'm looking forward to it."

"I'm... well, I'm starting to get my head around the idea. I have a tendency to be a bit negative whenever Frank springs into action, but I'll try to, er... embrace this endeavour. They're bound to realise that he's no pro though."

"I wouldn't be so sure about that. I think he's a pretty good actor himself."

"Yes," I said, storing that little nugget away for later. After all, anyone can operate a video camera.

The location which Marta had suggested struck us both as very atmospheric. As well as a pool almost entirely surrounded by rocks, there was an old bridge over a rocky outcrop, formerly used to transport minerals from the nearby mines to waiting boats. The views across the bay to the castle and the mountains beyond were splendid, and Diego and I scouted the best spots to film from, before he made a short and terribly amateur video on his phone and emailed it to Frank. We then sat on some rocks and watched a few bits of *Umberto D.*

"She does look a lot like Marta, but is that really good acting? Her and the old man just seem to be chatting like me and you," Diego said.

"I think that's the idea. This wasn't Hollywood, you see. I seem to remember it was called neorealism. Frank inflicted a lot of these old films on me back in the day and I didn't really appreciate them then. Maybe I'll like them more now that I'm older and wiser."

"It makes you think though, doesn't it? If amateur actors really can do it OK, and with the technology we've got these days, it might be possible for Frank to make a really good film."

"Yes, but not with a script he's knocked up in an afternoon. Come on, let's head back and give him a hand."

We found the great man hunched over the tiny table with a pen in his hand and the tip of his tongue sticking out.

"How's it going, Frank?" I said.

He held up his left hand and scribbled something with his right, before dropping the pen and throwing back his head.

"Ah, how I love an artistic deadline. I've never had one before and it really gets the creative juices flowing. I'm almost done now, I think, then we can read it through."

I peered over his shoulder. "I can hardly understand a word of it."

"No, one of you will have to nip out to buy some paper and a couple of pens. We're going to have to make three fair copies of this."

We both went and stopped off for a coffee to get our copying juices flowing. When we got back he was lying on his bed with his pad on his chest.

"I'm spent," he moaned. "An empty vessel."

"Have a nap," I said.

He pushed himself up. "No, I can't rest until the job's done. Right, I'll act it out. Diego, make notes if you like. Justin, you should understand most of it, as it's earthy, straightforward stuff. Pay particular attention to your own parts. One of you time it, please."

I'll spare you the script for now, save to say that Marta was in action most of the time, if action's the word, because she spent about four of the film's eleven-minute duration looking wistfully out to sea. My character is the first to interrupt her reverie, but not for long, as it turns out that I'm a deaf-mute.

"I thought it would simplify things and it gives Marta the chance to show her compassionate side, despite all her woes. Restart the clock."

After our muted exchange I wander away and Marta muses a bit more before Diego comes along, looking terribly upset and agitated. He stands on the edge of the cliff, staring down at the waves crashing against the rocks.

I stopped the timer on my phone. "Er, Frank, there aren't any cliffs there, just rocks."

"High enough to dash your head against one and drown?"

"Yes, I suppose so, if you aimed well."

"That'll do then. Start the clock."

Marta then strolls over and speaks calmly to him. Still on the perilous rocks, he explains that his girlfriend has just left him for another and he wishes to end it all. He, a humble florist, can't hope to compete against a man who owns a chain of butcher's shops.

"Note the symbolism there," said Frank.

Marta's simple, sincere words comfort him and she manages to lure him away from the 'precipice'. They go on talking and she reveals that her own life is far from perfect. She has an awful job in a cafe which she can't leave because she has to support her ailing father, and it slowly dawns on Diego how selfless his saviour is.

"Note the subtly of the dialogue. She downplays her own problems and only through Diego's facial expressions and posture do we know how profoundly he's been affected."

I glanced at Diego and his facial expression suggested that he doubted his ability to pull this off.

Marta and Diego go on exchanging a few words, but mostly gaze out to sea. We're led to believe that a hint of future love may be in the air, but just then Catalina arrives and scolds Marta, her employee, for spending too long away from the cafe. Marta meekly endures her harangue, including a threat to fire her, before Catalina stomps away, looking grim and avaricious. The film ends with a shot of Marta and Diego from behind, gazing out to sea.

"...then we fade out, and bang! My first ever short film's in the bag. So what do you reckon?"

"It's... it's interesting," I said.

"At least there aren't many lines to learn," said Diego. "It might be a bit, er... deep for me; to act, I mean."

"Nonsense, you just have to put yourself in your character's shoes, but don't overdo it. Before we film you'll have to spend ten minutes thinking about Emma."

"No, that'll just make me smile. It was such a relief when we split up."

"Hmm, have you ever loved and lost?"

"Not really. Well, there was a girl at school I fancied a lot, but she never paid any attention to me."

"She'll have to do. Justin, how do you feel about your part?"

"Happy with its brevity. I knew a deaf chap quite well once," I lied. "So I'll think about him."

"Good. Right, let's get this thing copied out, then we can relax."

"Er, Frank, would you like to hear a suggestion first?" said Diego.

He frowned. "What sort of suggestion?"

"Well, at the end, right at the end, I think they should reach out their hands, without even looking at each other, and sort of join their fingers."

I nodded. "Intertwine their fingers, yes, but just a couple, and then maybe let their hands fall by their sides, so we're left wondering if they'll get together or not."

Frank rubbed his chin, scratched his nose, then shook his head. "No, it's too unsubtle."

Diego and I argued our case for some kind of closure and he eventually agreed to at least let them touch hands briefly. "But I hope you're not expecting a writing credit for that bit of input."

I chuckled. "No, Frank."

"It's all your own work," said Diego. "Come on, let's copy it."

Half an hour later we had three fairly legible scripts with hardly any instructions, as Frank planned to give those on the day.

"Er, won't our actresses expect typed scripts, Frank?" I said. "They might suspect that this is something you knocked up in a couple of hours."

"I'll explain that I had to revise the original. Well done, lads. Dinner's on me."

Over our last supper before our acting and directorial debuts, Frank was full of plans for our future. Documentaries, he said, were all very well as a sideline, but independent feature films were the way to go. Now that we'd seen how easy it was to get people on board, he didn't see why we shouldn't write and produce a short film everywhere we went.

"We'll have a new creative adventure every time. We'll spend a day absorbing the atmosphere, then find our actors and write the film."

"In that order?" I said.

"Yes. All the great directors usually knew who they'd be working with beforehand, so we'll do the same."

"I agree," said Diego, who'd drunk a few glasses of wine. "If we only find an old man and a... a parrot to take part, for example, then we'll write the film for them, and us, of course."

I drummed my fingers on the terrace table. "Frank, I've noticed that the word 'we' is being bandied about a lot. Are Diego and me to be allowed to contribute more next time?"

He smiled. "I don't see why not. You both lack the extensive knowledge of world cinema that I possess, but that could work in our favour."

I thought about the similarities between *Umberto D.*, Frank's fictitious film for the Venice festival, and the one he'd just written. "Yes, I guess we might come up with some fresh ideas."

Frank raised his glass of *sin alcohol*. "Here's to the first of many collaborations."

We clinked glasses and drank.

"Let's be off," Frank said. "You two need to get your beauty sleep."

10

Since leaving Bilbao Airport behind we hadn't seen a drop of rain. This was unusual for the north of Spain and the clouds which had gathered the following morning suggested that our luck might be about to run out.

"Today of all days, damn it," said Frank as we walked towards our open-air film set.

Diego looked at his phone. "It's forecast to rain later. What'll we do if it starts pissing it down?"

"Soldier on, of course. I'll buy a brolly before tomorrow to protect the camera. We won't get cold anyway, and a bit of rain might add to the drama. Hmm, shame we can't turn it on when we want it."

Soon after we'd arrived at the picturesque natural pool, Marta and her mother pulled up on a nearby lane in a shiny red Audi TT.

"They must be quite well off," said Frank.

I chuckled. "They might be prepared to invest in your... our future projects."

"Hmm, I'll bear that in mind."

"I was joking."

"Many a true word... hola, Catalina, Marta! You're both looking great."

They seemed quite eager and I noticed that they'd brought hefty umbrellas and a large canvas bag which turned out to contain food and drink, something we'd overlooked, having forgotten to appoint a catering manager. Frank handed them each a copy of the script and explained its handwritten state.

"I had to revise it completely with you in mind." He clapped. "Right, we'll act it out right away. I'll give directions, but please save any questions for afterwards."

"Where's the camera?" Catalina asked.

"In my bag, with the tripod. I won't need them yet." He turned to me. "Justin, have a look around and find the most dangerous spot."

"It's there, past the old bridge."

We headed over and Frank told Marta what she'd have to do for about two minutes.

"Just look out to sea?"

"Yes, thinking deeply about your troubled life."

"But who am I?"

"You're a waitress, so the white blouse is perfect, and it'll look good against the cloudy sky. OK, you can begin." And thirty second later. "Just stop for a moment, Marta."

"But I'm not doing anything."

"Yes, you are. You're acting the part of a person who's looking out to sea and thinking, when what you have to do is just look out to sea and think. I'll be filming you in profile, so you can ruffle your brow a bit, but not all the time. OK, carry on."

His spiel carried a certain conviction and she did as she was told, while her mother looked proudly on.

"That's better, Marta. OK, so now Justin comes along and you say what's written there, then you realise he's deaf, so you try to communicate with him, doing a bit of miming. You show that you sympathise with his deafness and after a minute or so he walks away, looking happy to have met you. Right, have a go at that."

Marta read from her script. "Hello, it's such a lovely sunny day, and the sea is so calm." She looked up. "But it's cloudy and the sea's rather rough, Frank."

"Yes, say something like that then. It's just about making contact."

She said something like that and I smiled, raised my hands and pointed to my ears.

"Cut! I mean stop. Justin you're not playing a deaf-mute in a Buster Keaton film, you *are* a deaf-mute. Think about that deaf friend of yours and do it again."

So we did it again, and again, and again, and it gradually dawned on us that movie-making wasn't as easy as it looked, although Frank made a good job of appearing to have directed many times before. After about half an hour of improvisation he settled on a brief but warm exchange, after which Marta looked out to sea and went on brooding. I feared that her subsequent meeting with the suicidal lad might take us the rest of the day to rehearse to Frank's satisfaction, but right from the off Diego proved himself to be a natural. His agitated arrival, contorted face and stumbling gait were perfect, and as he'd already learnt his lines he was able to deliver them quite well. Marta seemed to feed off his performance, as we say in the trade, and greeted him with convincing concern. Had she known her lines I think they could have pulled it off quite soon, but the clouds were ever more ominous and Frank decided to move on to Catalina's scene, which was when his problems began.

She'd already read her lines and didn't like them one bit. She said a cafe proprietress would be highly unlikely to go clambering over rocks to fetch her tardy waitress, and if she did she wouldn't dare to abuse her in that way because in summer good employees were like gold dust on the coast and if she fired her she might not find another for a fortnight, so then where would she be? Besides, Castro Urdiales was a lovely place full of kindly people and after fourteen summers there she'd yet to meet such a witch of a woman.

Frank patiently heard her out. "Catalina, this is a film. It's fiction. Forget Castro Urdiales. We need your character so that Marta's character can show her stoical nature to Diego's character."

"But I could play her mother who comes to tell her that she's been fired. That would be when Diego realises that he isn't the only one with troubles."

"Her mother's dead," he said tersely. "That's why she has to support her poor father. Look, Catalina, I spent weeks writing this and I can't change it all now. We have to be in... Almería by Friday."

"Mamá, just do as you're told," said Marta.

"All right, but I think it's a rotten part to play."

"Perfect!" Frank cried.

"What?"

"That expression. Look, we'll come back one day and make a film with a much nicer part for you, but for now just try to stay annoyed. I know being nasty isn't in your nature, but hold that frame of mind. All right, Marta, Diego, look out to sea. Approach her, Catalina, and give her a piece of your mind."

To my untrained eyes she performed well and had she known her lines Frank could have gone ahead and filmed the scene. All that remained was the final shot of Marta and Diego looking out to sea, just for a change, and Frank decided to allow their fingers to stay entwined right till the end.

"That was great. Thank you, thank you, all of you," he gushed.

"Let's have some lunch," said Catalina. "Then we can learn our lines and get filming."

Frank chuckled. "It's a little more difficult than you may think, Catalina. First I'll have to study the light and the angles, and then we'll have to do many takes."

"As you wish, but it's going to rain all day tomorrow."

We all looked at Frank.

He scratched his head. "We'll see. Thanks for bringing the food. I... I was going to take you to a restaurant."

We made ourselves reasonably comfortable on the rocks and tucked into the delicious pasties and little *bocadillos*, washed down with beer or water, followed by coffee from a big flask and some dainty cakes.

"We'll bring all this next time," Frank said to me in English.

"Yes, we should."

"What do you think of it so far?"

"I... I'm not sure. I'm a bit hopeless, but Diego's great and they're pretty good too. Let's get some of it filmed, shall we? Just in case," I said, keen to get my brief intervention out of the way.

"All right, we'll try."

He gave us half an hour to learn our lines – more than enough for me – and stalked off to study the light and the angles.

By the time Marta resumed her now familiar stance on the rocks a series of black clouds were rolling in from the sea. Frank had placed the larger of his two microphones between two stones near her feet and much to my relief my scene was 'a wrap' after only three takes. After viewing the footage he told the others to try to project their voices down towards the mic, but to avoid looking at it.

He repositioned the tripod. "Right, Marta, another minute of looking out to sea, then I'll pan onto Diego. When he's arrived I'll cut and come and film from another angle. OK, scene two, take one and... action!"

Diego stumbled over the rocks like a man at the end of his tether and shuffled to a halt a couple of yards from Marta.

"Cut! That's brilliant, but we'll do it again, just in case."

After another successful take the light rain that began to fall promised to be a mere prelude to the sheets of it that were already visible across the bay. Frank moved the camera and told them to start right away. They began well, then Marta fluffed her lines.

"Sorry, the rain's putting me off."

The ever-thoughtful Catalina had opened an umbrella and was already protecting Frank and the tools of his trade from the rain, which had increased in intensity. I opened the other one.

"OK, do it again and if you forget what to say, just improvise. You two have a certain compenetration by now and I think you'll manage it."

Diego wiped his brow and winked at me.

Frank filmed up to the point where Catalina was due to appear and said it might be good enough.

"OK, Justin, leave that umbrella and come and hold this one."

"Can I dry my hair?" said a bedraggled Marta.

"Of course not. You have to look the same."

"My mum's hair's still dry."

"Hmm, that's true. Catalina, by the time you get over there it should be wet enough."

"Can I not use the umbrella?"

"Afraid not. You'll need both hands to gesticulate with." He gave her a gentle shove. "Off you go. OK, and once again improvise if you have to. Right, scene four, take one, and... action!"

Catalina looked even more annoyed this time around and gave her employee a real tongue-lashing.

"Cut! No, sorry, that's too much, Catalina. You looked like you were about to murder her."

"I feel like murdering someone."

"It was your idea to start filming. Please go back over there. Remember, you're a nasty, selfish woman, but you're not a homicidal maniac."

This time Catalina seethed but didn't quite boil over and after their second attempt Frank said it was almost perfect. Me being the only other dry person there, I agreed that another attempt might be worthwhile. The rain was hammering down by now and the three players looked a sorry sight, but with true professionalism they did the scene again, but with poorer results.

"I think the last take was good enough," said Frank. "Right, this last scene should be easy. Thanks, Catalina. You can get under the umbrella now."

"What the hell for?" she said, before pushing back her sodden locks and laughing.

Frank and I moved behind Marta and Diego for the final silent scene and when their fingers had remained entwined for a minute or so he switched off the camera.

"That's it, we've done it!" he cried, before rushing off to hug his actors and soon becoming as wet as them. I stayed put to protect the gear and reflected that however the film turned out, they'd certainly given it their best shot in such appalling conditions.

It must have been my lucky day, because when the time came to hand back the brolly the rain had stopped. Our actresses were eager to get back to their apartment, so after arranging to meet for dinner at nine we waved them off. Just then the sun popped out and illuminated Frank's already radiant face.

"Ah, it's a great feeling to have brought my first proper film project to fruition."

"Shouldn't we come back tomorrow to try to improve each scene?" I said.

"Oh, no, we wouldn't do it any better and the rain might not be the same. It's only a first attempt, after all, so we'll have to be happy with what we've got."

Back in the room Frank was reluctant to give us a glimpse of what we'd got, saying that we ought to let it mature for a while and come back to it with fresh eyes.

"What clapcrap," said Diego.

"Claptrap," I said.

"Thanks. What claptrap, Frank. It's not going to get any better."

So we huddled together on Frank's bed and watched our unedited efforts on the little screen. I'd expected it to be pretty amateurish, but it wasn't bad at all. He'd got the light right most of the time and the sound was reasonably good. The image quality ranged from extremely clear to only slightly blurred and the camera juddered just a couple of times. Our acting came across better than I'd anticipated, even mine, but the film's real strong point was the way the rain increased as the action reached its 'climax'. Even the insipid little story carried more weight when seen on the screen, and I resolved to try to come up with a new story for our next effort.

"That's all, folks," said Frank. He switched off the camera and cradled it. "It'll look much better when it's edited and I've added some suitable background music. I'll make some titles too, so I must ask them their last names. Ah, when we get home I'll have my work cut out, as I expect we'll have done a few of these films by then. I think I'll make an anthology, and maybe slip in the interviews too, or maybe not."

"Er, I've enjoyed today," I said. "But I want to do more things than just make films on our trip."

Diego frowned. "Like what?"

"Well, sightseeing and walking and things."

Frank squeezed my shoulder. "That goes without saying, Justin, but we'll always be on the lookout for new actors and locations. That's far better than bumbling around like aimless, gawping tourists, don't you think?"

I shrugged and stood up. "Time will tell." I remembered Diego's little nugget. "I think you should have a go at acting too, Frank. I think you'd be good at it, and one of us could film those scenes."

"Yes, it has crossed my mind, but cameramen are made, not born, you know. It's a tremendously steep learning curve."

I recalled the daft things he'd made me do back in Blackburn, by the canal locks, near the cathedral, and even in the shopping mall until a security guard had hustled us out.

"We can try. Blackburn seems like another world now, doesn't it?"

"I have a few fond memories," said Diego. "But I doubt I'll ever go back."

"My days are numbered there," said Frank. "I mean to put my affairs in order, kiss my mother goodbye till my next visit, and be on another plane to Bilbao before you can say *cuchillo*."

"Knife," I said. "I pick up more Spanish when we're with other folk."

Frank grinned. "Rest assured that we'll be spending lots of time with other folk from now on."

"How do you feel about Blackburn now, Justin?" Diego said in Spanish.

"Er, I don't want to live there anymore. I prefer Spain now. I also want to go home and..." I switched to English. "...put my affairs in order, I think."

Frank smiled. "Of course you do. You've been hooked for a while now."

"No, I think it was meeting Marta and her mum that did it. The way they just went along with your plans and were so open and friendly."

"And the food they brought," said Diego.

"Yes, that too. I can't imagine anything like that ever happening back home. I hadn't made a new friend in years until I met you. Unless something happens to really put me off, I don't think I'll be back in Blackburn for long either."

Diego shook his head. "You're both hopeless cases, so I'll stop trying to persuade you to go home and get jobs, as I can see it isn't going to happen. Instead I'll try to help you not to become beggars within a few years."

"Thanks, Diego," I said.

"There's plenty of work in Ólvega, you know, for those who have the right contacts."

"Thanks, Diego," said Frank. "We mustn't rule anything out at this stage."

"So when will we be able to see the film?" Catalina asked over our supper of tapas in a busy bar by the harbour.

"Oh, I'll send it to you in October, I think," said Frank. "I'll have a lot of work to do on it before then. Did you ever get round to having a look at *Umberto D.*, by the way?"

Marta chuckled. "Yes, we watched a few scenes. I remembered you saying that the girl was an amateur actress and I think that helped me when we started today."

"And I saw that you'd based my part on that awful landlady, you rogue," said Catalina. "I want to play someone more like myself next time, if there is a next time."

"When do you leave for Almería?" Marta asked him.

He smiled. "We're not actually going there. I exaggerated my film experience a bit to persuade you to take part."

Catalina grinned at her daughter. "I told you so. Venice Film Festival indeed! I mean, no food, no vehicle, no umbrellas." She looked at Frank. "I knew it was just a hobby of yours, but I don't mind."

Frank smiled. "Something more than a hobby, my dear Catalina, but one must start somewhere."

"You'll be surprised how good the film is," I said loyally.

"If you come back here I'd like to act again too," said Marta with what might have been a meaningful look at Diego, who sat by her side.

I engaged Catalina in conversation so that the co-stars could have a quiet little chat and Diego seemed to make the most of the opportunity. Marta was twelve years younger than him, but he'd told me that such an age difference was quite common in Spain, so I wondered if he was trying to woo her with a view to a future liaison or simply enjoying his last hour with the pretty girl.

Catalina insisted on footing the bill, and after exchanging numbers and emails we wished them goodbye until the visit we hoped to make the following year.

"And don't forget to look at the weather forecast before your next film," was Catalina's parting shot when they turned to wave from the corner.

"I would like to see them again," I said after we'd ordered a final drink.

"Me too," said Frank. "I shouldn't think we'll end up living too far from here, and Ólvega isn't a million miles away."

"How far is it?" I asked a pensive Diego.

"About 286 kilometres."

I chuckled. "About?"

"I looked it up, but I shan't be coming, if that's what you're thinking. She's studying in Madrid and she has a boyfriend."

"Boyfriends come and go," I said. "You should at least stay in touch."

"I might, but in any case I can't see any future there. She's going to be a teacher and she'll have to go where the work is. I want someone who'll be happy to live in Ólvega."

Frank chuckled. "You might get bored of it, just like we got bored of Blackburn."

"No, we're not the same as you. When Spaniards go somewhere to work they almost always want to go home eventually. Our families and our towns mean more to us than you." He sighed. "If I can find a nice girl from Ólvega we'll both be happier. So, this is our last night in our cosy room. Shall we move on tomorrow?"

"Yes, I think so," I said. "Where next?"

"Along the coast past Santander to a little place called Comillas."

"How far is that?"

"About 112 kilometres, but it's back to camping, I'm afraid. The cheap hotels are all booked up."

"That's fine," said Frank. "I'm fed up of sleeping with the pair of you anyway."

"Diego, do you feel up to sharing a tent now?" I said.

He sighed. "I guess so."

"The screenwriter should have his own tent," said Frank.

"That's fine by me," I said.

"Is it?"

"Yes, because I'm going to write our next script, with a little help from my friends to translate it into Spanish, of course."

"Let's toss up for it. The tent, I mean."

We tossed a euro coin and I lost.

"Bad luck, mate."

"At the next place then."

Diego then told us that a wholly coastal route would mean missing some splendid mountains, so after Comillas we'd be nipping inland to the Picos de Europa.

"Suits me," said Frank. "There's no need to lie on the beach every day, and the mountains will broaden our cinematic horizons."

11

There was no prospect of lying on the beach the next day because it didn't stop raining until just after we'd pitched the tents at about six o'clock. We'd decided we oughtn't to bypass every single city and had spent a few damp hours in Santander, visiting the Museum of Prehistory and the futuristic Centro Botín art gallery in order to stay under cover. We agreed that it must be a lovely city in the sunshine, but felt that we'd fulfilled our quota of conurbations for the time being. Part of the campsite at Comillas was perched on some low cliffs and had superb views across the bay and out to sea, but much to Frank's annoyance this field was full of motorhomes, while mere tent-dwellers had to make do with one of several small and mostly shadeless fields a little further inland.

"It's bloody typical," he said as we hammered in the last pegs.

"Yes, it was bound to stop raining as soon as we finished," I said.

"No, I mean letting the motorised campers have the best spot."

I pointed at the car. "Er, we're motorised campers too, Frank."

"You know what I mean."

"And did you notice that a few had British number plates?"

"And a couple of cars over there too," said Diego.

"Oh, I don't mind British tourists."

"You said we wouldn't see any in the north," I said.

"I meant expats, not tourists. It's too wet for the sun-worshipping, beer-guzzling layabouts up here. The expats come to Spain to fry what's left of their brains, while these tourists at least show a little discernment by choosing to come to Comillas. I believe Gaudí designed one of his first architectural marvels here. We'll have to go and see that."

A while later we walked into town and admired the many houses which sported the typical Cantabrian wooden balconies on the upper floors. We did a little shopping, then decided to have dinner at a cheapish place near the new town hall rather than cooking and eating on the damp grass. The town was full of tourists and several languages could be heard, including English, so Frank insisted on speaking Spanish for a change. Diego proved to be a considerate tent companion, so I was able to dispense with my earplugs at last.

The next morning we hit the tourist trail, visiting Gaudí's quirky villa with its weird tower and amazing mosaics, the stunning neo-Gothic Palacio de Sobrellano, and the impressive Pontifical University. I was surprised to discover that these and several other notable buildings had been constructed in the late nineteenth century. After a little research I found that this was down to the friendship of King Alfonso XII with a shipping magnate called Antonio López, on whom he bestowed the title of Marquis of Comillas. When the king agreed to visit in 1881 the new marquis made extensive preparations, including the first ever electric street lamps used in Spain, and after the great event the town went from strength to strength. The second marquis finished the university which his soon defunct father had planned and because he was pally with the modern architects of Barcelona, one called Joan Martorell came to build the palace, followed by Gaudí, and last but not least, in Frank's opinion, Lluís Domènech i

Montaner, who before going on to design some great buildings in Barcelona did something very odd to the old cemetery by the sea.

At the time the cemetery surrounded a sixteenth century church which had been abandoned early on due to a falling-out over seating arrangements. They went on burying folk there, but the church was allowed to crumble in the midst of the tombs, so when in 1893 Domènech – who had already had a hand in the palace and the university – was asked to expand the place, the fellow got a bit carried away and let his imagination run riot. Believing, in my opinion, that no-one would give a hoot what he did to the tumbledown place near the cliffs, he built a showy neo-Gothic arch at the entrance and topped his new surrounding walls with a series of curious pinnacles. He then invited his friend, the Catalan sculptor Josep Llimona, to have a go at designing some new tombs for the rich folk, including an awesome marble one representing waves with an angel looking over them.

The sculpture which got Frank going was another angel which hadn't actually fit into its intended mausoleum – these sculptors are no architects, you see – so they ended up shoving it on top of an old arch, little knowing, I suspect, how famous it would become. Frank, by then a little jaded by all our sightseeing, spotted it right away.

"El Ángel Exterminador!" he exclaimed as soon as we'd passed through the wrought iron gates.

"What?"

"Look, The Exterminating Angel, the sculpture famous for inspiring Buñuel's great film of the same name." He pointed up at a marble woman with wings. "I knew it was up north somewhere, but fancy us finding it here." He gazed around at the six-tier, marble-clad burial niches, then led us under another arch to the flashy tombs. "Oh, we just *have* to make a film here."

"Er, there must be thirty people here right now, all looking very much like tourists," I said.

"But it doesn't close till eight. It's bound to be quiet later on, and no-one seems to be in charge. Oh, it's such an eerie place to make a film."

"Yes, it is atmospheric," said Diego.

"An opportunity not to be missed," said Frank.

Diego chuckled. "Justin, you said you were going to write the next script, so you'd better get cracking."

"Oh, this is too... too limiting. I wouldn't know where to start."

"Look, someone has to write the script and someone has to find the actors," said Frank. "Which would you rather do?"

"Write the script, but what about Diego?"

"I'm a jack of all trades. I'll help you both."

Frank looked at his watch. "It's half past one. By tomorrow at six we have to be here, ready to rehearse, so we'd better get our skates on."

I protested that this was a silly way of putting needless pressure on ourselves, to which Frank countered by saying that we'd already seen the sights and I'd have plenty of time to write the script on the beach that afternoon.

"And the actors?"

"Leave them to me. As for the script, think Gothic, sinister, maybe some kind of horror story. The sun will be quite low in the evening, so imagine the shadows we'll be able to use."

I felt cornered, but spotted an escape route. "But we need to know who'll be in it before I can write it."

Frank pushed me toward the gates. "Come on, let's grab some lunch back at the site and then go and find them."

"You go ahead. I need to get some inspiration here first."

As I was wandering around taking snaps on my phone, a young chap with a badge on began to usher people out. Clutching at a not unpromising straw, I asked him in halting Spanish if he'd mind us filming there.

"Many people filming here on their phones," he replied in English.

"No, I mean with a proper film camera. We want to make a short film here, with actors, in the evening before you close. I suppose that's not allowed."

He chuckled. "Do as you wish. It is quiet later. Come, I must lock up now."

As I strolled back along the promenade I racked my brain for at least the seed of an idea for the film, but had come up with nothing when I reached the tent and found Frank making sandwiches.

"Where's Diego?"

"Over there, talking to a pair of our compatriots. He was admiring their shiny van and they got chatting. Any ideas yet?"

"Nope. Any actors yet?"

"Of course not. I'll stalk up and down the beach later and see if I like the look of anyone."

I asked him if he'd settle for an interview with the young custodian of the cemetery. "He seems friendly enough. He said we could film there anyway."

"It was a good idea to ask him," he said, his smile implying that he knew the reason why. "I think I've got an idea you could work on."

"Let me have it."

Frank was outlining some nonsense about a man making a pact with the devil when Diego came over with a handsome couple in their forties.

"Guys, meet Yvonne and Craig. They're from Scotland."

Frank's lips curled up on hearing this, because, he told me later, he'd feared they might be smarmy English gits in a posh VW van like that. Far from being smarmy, they were both softly spoken teachers from Dundee who were spending their entire summer holiday in northern Spain.

Frank nobly offered them a tuna and tomato butty.

"No, thanks, we've already eaten," said Craig, a tall, fit-looking chap with a very un-Scottish tan. "Diego was saying that you were looking for a couple of actors for a short film you're making."

"Er, yes, but it's going to be in Spanish."

He smiled. "That's a shame. Ours isn't very good yet."

"Yes, we might have been up for it," said Yvonne, who resembled someone Frank couldn't quite put his finger on.

"You know," he said, grimacing and nipping the skin at the top of his nose, to aid thought, I believe. "You remind me of an actress who Bergman used a lot in his early films. Not the commercial ones he started out doing, but those in the fifties when he... ha! I've got it! Yes, you look a lot like Harriet Andersson. Have any of you seen *Summer with Monika*?"

We hadn't, or if he'd made me watch it years ago I'd forgotten about it.

"*Smiles of a Summer Night*?"

We shook our heads.

"*Sawdust and Tinsel*, *Dreams*, *Through a Glass Darkly*?"

We regretted that we hadn't.

"I know he was Swedish and is still very highly regarded," said Yvonne, scoring an appreciated but unnecessary brownie point, because Frank had already pencilled her in as his starring actress in the upcoming film which I dearly hoped he wasn't going to bullshit about, because they didn't look nearly as gullible as Catalina and Marta had seemed but turned out not to be.

"The film we're working on can just as easily be in English, I suppose," he said. "Would you be able to learn some lines tomorrow and be ready to rehearse at six?"

Craig grinned. "Both of us?"

"Oh, yes. There's a couple in it, you see, who meet a… an as yet not completely defined character, in that old cemetery here in town. We've already got permission to film there, and in three days' time we have to…" He spotted my frown. "…go to the Picos de Europa, for a break. We've just made a short feature in Castro Urdiales, you see, but we fancy using the cemetery here, so it's a race against time really."

"Brilliant," said Yvonne, whose face was starting to ring a bell, so I probably had seen at least one of those subtitled, black and white films. "We're heading that way soon too. We're looking for a house to buy, you see."

"As a summer home?" Diego asked.

"No, to live there." She giggled, probably like Harriet Andersson did, or still does, as she's still alive at the time of writing. "We plan to retire at fifty, three years from now, and try to live off the land."

"Live cheaply, anyhow," said Craig. "We've no kids, you see, so if we're wise with our money we should be able to make a go of it."

I nodded and looked at Frank, curious to see his reaction to this proposed invasion of his supposedly Brit-free cherished land.

He beamed. "Snap! Justin and me are looking for a place in the north too, though we'll probably rent somewhere initially."

"It's still a very vague idea," I muttered.

"In the sense that we haven't yet decided on an area," he countered.

"Or worked out how they're going to make a living," Diego added.

"Where are you up to with your house search?" I asked Yvonne and Craig.

"Please go ahead and eat," Craig said, before they filled us in on their proposed route, gradually west towards Galicia, and the type of property they were after, ideally somewhere with a few acres and not too far from the nearest village. Being polite folk, they then subtly enquired about our circumstances, so we told them what we'd done with our lives up to press. Yvonne felt sure that Frank would find at least a few hours of classes in any decent-sized village, as the Spanish had been English-mad ever since the last recession had forced many of them, like Diego, to seek work overseas. I then had cause to silently curse the amiable Craig, because he said that an experienced bookkeeper could surely make quite a bit of money by working online.

"You might not be able to be a company's actual bookkeeper if you're in Spain, but I think that larger firms might well take you on to do specific tasks. Once you start with one you'll be in a stronger position, and I'm sure that a bit of networking on LinkedIn and other sites will pay off."

My response to this very sound advice was to mutely acknowledge his input, while Frank's delight must have seemed disproportionate to them.

"Of course, of course!" he cried, slapping his remote bookkeeping buddy on the back, causing me to eject a soggy bit of bread. "Sorry. Yes, that's exactly what he should do. Had you not thought of that, Justin?"

I shrugged. "It had crossed my mind, but it might not be so easy. I mean, why employ someone who's over a thousand miles away when there are plenty of capable folk at home?"

"You could probably undercut most UK freelancers," said the well-meaning Scot.

"Your living costs probably won't be as high as theirs," said another.

"You should start looking into it right away," said that devil Diego, who knew full well why I'd kept the idea to myself.

"I'm in no hurry. Like you two, I may well retire at fifty, three and a half years from now."

"Cobblers," said Frank. "Time waits for no man. I bet Craig and Yvonne are only hanging in there till fifty so they'll get their teaching pensions, isn't that right?"

"No, we'll get nothing until we're fifty-five," said Yvonne. "So we'll have to keep costs down until then. We might well do a few English classes too."

"You see?" Frank said to me.

"What?" I croaked, wondering what sort of abstruse logic he was about to employ.

"They're taking a leap into the unknown just like us."

"I haven't leapt anywhere yet," I muttered.

Frank chucked and looked at the bemused couple. "Justin suffers from cold feet from time to time, but he's just as convinced as I am really."

Yvonne smiled wryly. "I wouldn't pressure him if I were you, Frank. We're a couple and have a joint aim in life, but a pair of friends, however close, shouldn't commit themselves to anything too limiting."

I could have jumped up and kissed her, but I just said that we ought to be going to the beach. Fortunately Yvonne and Craig were off to see the Gaudí house, because the small matter of the film script was still in my in-tray. Frank suggested that they also drop in at the cemetery, to get a feel for it. They agreed to go and invited us to their van for supper.

Our impending task diverted Frank from my future as a bookkeeping breadwinner, and no sooner had we settled down on our towels than he began to usurp my role as chief screenwriter. The couple, he suggested, ought to be having some sort of deep discussion, possibly near the marble tomb shaped like waves, when a man dressed in white approaches from the shadows.

"We don't have any white clothes," I said.

"I've got a white shirt and cream trousers, so I... whoever plays the part can wear them. So, this seemingly friendly chap says something or does something a bit disturbing and you sort of take it from there."

I smeared sun cream on my nose. "Right."

"You could, for instance, have him say something seemingly irrelevant, but which later turns out to be crucial, or, on the other hand, he might say something seemingly crucial which later turns out to be a red herring. Then again..."

I grabbed the notepad and dropped it on his balls.

"Ow!"

"Make a start, Frank. Coming for a swim, Diego?"

"Yep."

So off we went, and despite the chilly water we managed to swim right across the bay to the lighthouse and back again, before having a rest and then completing another smaller loop. When fatigue forced us back to Frank's side he'd already written most of the dialogue, as this too was going to be a film with plenty of pensive pauses, just like many of the great Bergman's masterpieces.

"So the man is actually a ghost," I said after reading it through.

"Yes, an ethereal being anyway, though they don't find out until the end when he walks through the wall."

Diego almost choked on his banana. "How are you going to manage that, Frank?"

"I'm not sure yet. Maybe in post-processing, or by sort of walking past a wall as if I'm... he's going through it, or a bit of both."

I felt yet more weight slipping from my shoulders. "I think you should play the ghost, Frank."

"Yes, I think you'd do it best," said Diego.

"Me? Oh, I... well, it had crossed my mind, but either of you could play it too. Diego, your slightly Spanish accent might heighten the drama, but then again it might not. Justin, your greying hair would come across quite well, and that haunted look you sometimes have for no apparent reason could be useful, but I'm not sure your heart would be in it."

I smiled. "That's settled then. Besides, we both need to practise our camerawork, because I'm sure you'll want to act in other films too."

He sighed and shook his head to conceal his grin. "Oh boy, I'm going to have my work cut out. Writing the thing, acting in it, and teaching you two how to film."

I squeezed his thigh. "It's your vocation, Frank. Right, read it out and we'll see if we can polish it up a bit."

When we met Yvonne and Craig at eight we were able to give them a fairly clean copy of the provisional script. Over our tasty supper of omelette, fried chicken and salad, Frank read it out between mouthfuls.

"And how are you going to walk through the wall, Frank?" Yvonne said after listening patiently to ten minutes of melodramatic gibberish.

Not having wasted the late afternoon snoozing in his tent as Diego and I had done, he told them that it was easy enough to do on video editing software. "I'll just sort of jump at the wall, then make myself disappear when I edit it, but we'll also film another shot of me walking *past* a wall, just in case. I'm still learning about stuff like that, though I've already done a few interesting interviews."

"You could show them..." Diego began, but Frank was already on his feet and off across the field for the camera.

We had a good postprandial laugh at Diego's granny's monologue, Señor Revilla's furious outburst, and Andoni's mundane chatter and swaying willy, before watching his more orthodox interviews with the pilgrims until the German lady was abruptly silenced.

"It's such a shame the battery ran out, or you could have seen her fanatical outburst and the lousy priests trying to drive me away. I shan't let that happen again."

Craig, not content at having enlightened Frank regarding my earning potential, now proceeded to swell his already more than healthy ego.

"I think it's great what you're doing, Frank. Although we've been laughing at your early mishaps, we could see how your interview technique kept improving, and now you've made your first short film too. We all have our hobbies, but I think it's brilliant when someone really gets their teeth into something new and tries to make go of it." Frank shrugged modestly. "We really want to give farming a go when we come to live here. My great-grandfather was a farmer up on the edge of the Cairngorms, but my granddad settled in Dundee and opened a hardware shop." He shrugged and sipped his beer. "I'm hoping it's still in my blood. We'll probably start with a few sheep and see how it goes. I don't know why, but your film-making really inspires me to live my own dream."

"We'd like to have a few alpacas too," said Yvonne. "Although the locals might laugh at us."

Frank the Pioneer waved his finger. "Don't let *anyone* stop you from doing what you want to do, Yvonne. That's my motto anyway. These two were just a *tiny* bit cynical at first, but they're slowly realising that there's method in my... not madness, but my overwhelming urge to test myself."

They've already had a taste of your madness in the bizarre little film you've signed them up for, I thought but didn't say.

"You'll be a great director one day," I said but didn't think.

He shrugged. "I doubt I'll be a really great one, but like Craig says, it's all about pushing oneself to greater heights."

"Have you started looking at houses online?" Diego asked them before Frank could start soliloquising.

It transpired that they'd done quite a lot of research and believed they could buy a smallholding with good pastureland for under two-hundred thousand.

"The house might need work, but we can't afford to spend more than that and the land is our priority," said Yvonne. "Without land there are some real bargains to be had all over the north, but especially inland to the west of here, as Catalonia and the Basque Country are quite dear."

"Soria's cheap," said Diego. "Except Ólvega."

"Yes, we thought about Soria, but we need somewhere with good grazing," said Craig.

"Er, what sort of bargains are to be had without land, Yvonne?" Frank said.

She told us that small, run-down houses in out of the way places were on sale for as little as twenty thousand, but that structurally sound ones could be had for fifty or sixty thousand.

"I think at that price most of them will need modernising, but if you're good at DIY you should be able to do most of the work yourselves," she said.

Frank smiled. "Justin's a dab hand at DIY."

"Am I?"

"Yes, don't you remember when you helped me to paper my room years ago? You ended up doing most of it and I'm sure you've gone from strength to strength since then. You've been a married householder, after all, while I always rented during my dissipated years in Spain."

"I only ever did basic stuff," I said, although given the right tools I was in fact a decent handyman. "Our very, very provisional plan is to rent anyway."

"You'd be better off buying a place," said the dastardly Diego. "You buy a house, do it up, then if things don't work out you'll have gained rather than lost. Renting is just throwing money away."

"That's right," said Craig.

"Buying makes more sense," said Yvonne.

I saw Frank's eyes twinkling in the lamplight, so I yawned and prepared to beat a retreat.

"Brilliant!" he yelped. "Yes, yes, don't you see that it'd only cost us thirty grand each, Justin? That's peanuts and we'd still have plenty of money left."

"We'd better get to the cemetery first thing tomorrow and think about where we're going to film," I said.

"I could ask my granny about houses for sale in Deza, if you like," Diego said with a diabolical grin.

"Let's focus on the task at hand," I said.

Frank was already swiping and jabbing his phone like a man possessed. "You're right, Yvonne. I'm looking at a random part of Asturias and the house prices start at next to nothing. Ha, we could even snap one up before we go home."

Becoming annoyed by this blatant disregard for my autonomy, when Yvonne came to the rescue I blessed the white cotton socks she was wearing.

"Not so fast, Frank. You oughtn't to rush into these things and Justin looks far from convinced. Just look around for now and have a cooling off period once you get home."

I nodded. "Yes, yes, a long one."

"And you have to remember that it's summer now," said Craig. "It's quite cold and very wet here in winter. That's all right for sheep, but it isn't for everyone."

"Bah, it can't be as cold as back home," said Frank.

Craig, who was growing on me, then pointed out that in modern Britain we didn't know the meaning of the word cold anymore, as everyone had central heating. In the north of Spain most prosperous people had it too, but an old house in a village certainly wouldn't.

"So you either have to be tough and manage with a stove and heaters, or factor central heating into your costs," he concluded.

Frank rubbed his knuckles. "We're both pretty tough."

"My granny manages without central heating," said Diego.

"And she's ancient," said Frank.

"Maybe, but she's used to it. I bet you'll suffer more, Frank, having lived in the south of Spain for so long," said my pal Craig. "In fact you should come out in winter to look for a house, then you'll see what the score is."

"That's right," said Yvonne.

"Yes, it is," I said, reasoning that once we were back in Blackburn Frank's persuasive powers would diminish. I performed a yawn. "Bedtime for me, I think."

Frank's complacent gaze seemed to say that while four layers of tent fabric might separate us during the coming nights, the rest of the time I'd be at his mercy.

The following day was all about the film and Frank was shrewd enough to leave the matter of the house purchase to simmer in our subconscious minds. When the young chap came to open the cemetery at ten we were already waiting at the splendidly crafted gates and we had half an hour of relative peace to make up our minds where to film Frank's latest masterpiece, provisionally and preposterously entitled, *The Exterminating Angel II*.

"What's the film we made in Castro Urdiales going to be called?" Diego asked him as we strolled back to the campsite.

"Oh, *Monika*, I think."

"Why?"

"Well, we didn't give anyone names, so Marta can be Monika, which was Harriet Andersson's name in *Summer with Monika*. That way when discerning folk see it, they'll put two and two together and see it as a modest homage to Bergman, just like this one."

I pictured poor Ingmar turning in his grave. "These rush jobs are all very well, Frank, but wouldn't it be better to settle down to write something a bit more... well, substantial?"

"Of course, but the cemetery was simply crying out to be used. We've all got a lot to learn, but practice, practice, practice is the name of the game," he said, before putting us through an hour of intensive camera practice back at the site, much to the bemusement or amusement of the other campers.

"Frank," I said after he'd made me film him entering and leaving his tent for the fourth time. "This thing has autofocus and it reads the light. A child... no, a baby could use it if it was strong enough to press the button."

"Maybe, but babies aren't born with a knowledge of exposure compensation, are they? Right, Diego, your turn."

After a hasty lunch Diego and I went to the beach, while Frank stayed behind to learn his lines. When we got back, not only had he learnt them, but he'd written another ghostly monologue and learnt that too.

I read it. "Frank, this is like Hamlet on LSD or something. I suppose it'll sound all right with all this alliteration and whatnot, but it's basically a load of waffle."

"He likes the sound of his own voice," said Diego, whose tan had already surpassed anything the most ardent sun-worshipping Brit could ever hope to achieve.

Frank grinned. "That's right. I just want to see how it comes across."

"Yvonne and Craig are going to feel like bloody stooges," I said.

"Oh, they won't mind. It's a new experience for them." He looked at his watch. "Right, time for a nap now. We all need to be in tiptop shape for the filming."

"They're only expecting to rehearse today," I said.

"They know their lines and they'll be fine. I'll wake you at five."

We took our mats into the shade and obediently fell asleep.

The filming was a short, sharp reality check for the budding director and leading actor. Our Castro Urdiales effort was a work of unparalleled genius compared to *The Exterminating Angel II*, soon to be renamed *That Ghastly Cock-up in Comillas* by Frank himself. The opening scene started off well enough, as Yvonne and Craig played a man and wife talking quite naturally about how spooky the cemetery was, but when they began to discuss the merits of the statue on the arch and the significance of The Exterminating Angel in the bible, including references to the Book of Revelation, even their best efforts couldn't make their contrived and pretentious lines ring true. Then, when Diego and I were setting up for scene two, Frank nipped around the corner and refused to reveal himself until we started filming, whereupon he appeared to the couple from behind a tomb, his hair and face plastered with talcum powder. Instead of the expressions of shock and awe that we were intended to capture, all four of us burst out laughing, and we even heard the attendant guffawing behind the wall.

After that it went from bad to worse. Frank's first little speech, though weakly written and hammily delivered, made a modicum of sense, but his second one was not so much a flight of fancy as a dive into excruciating drivel. Try as they might, Yvonne and Craig just couldn't manage the terrified countenances required by the script, being so dumbfounded by this unexpected new monologue that they looked like a couple patiently hearing out a double-glazing salesman on their doorstep. In the last scene, after Frank had thrown himself against a wall and not even bothered to request a second shot of him walking *past* one, just in case the special effects didn't work out, Yvonne and Craig slowly recovered – this wasn't difficult – before reflecting on how the ghostly apparition had changed their concept of reality and their relationship with the world and each other, etc. etc. *ad nauseam*, until Diego was finally able to cry, "Cut! It's a wrap, I think."

"Now is five to eight," said the lurking attendant, and we couldn't get out of there fast enough.

"A kind of crazy comedy, eh?" the lad said to me as I brought up the rear.

"Yes, you could say that. Thanks for letting us film."

"No problem. Your friend with the *polvo de talco* on the head, he shit actor, no?"

"He tried his best," I said loyally. "Buenas tardes."

"The thing is," Craig said on the terrace of a cafe near the neat little port once Frank had returned after dunking his head in the sink. "It doesn't do to be too ambitious at this stage. That other film was a simple little drama that worked quite well, but I think you tried to cram too much into this one."

Frank sighed. "To be honest, Craig, although I'm really grateful for your collaboration in that... that *thing*, I'd rather talk about our common interest, house buying."

"No!" I said more loudly than I'd intended. "We shouldn't just sweep it under the carpet. We need to discuss what went wrong and what went... not quite so wrong."

"It's simple," said Frank. "Whereas I had a flash of inspiration before I wrote *Monika*, this time I tried to force it too much. We won't make another film until we've written a really good script. Then and only then will we look for our actors."

"Yes, we ought to get writing right away," I said.

Frank shook his head ominously. "No, Justin, we need to refresh our weary minds by thinking about something completely different. We have our whole lives ahead of us to make films, but only a few weeks to find a house in which to base ourselves while we make them."

An imploring look brought Yvonne to the rescue. "We're going to a site in Asturias near a village called Arenas de Cabrales tomorrow. Why don't you come along and we'll do some good hikes together." She glanced at me and almost winked. "Up in the mountains, miles from anywhere."

"Yes, we'll do that," I said.

"Sounds like a plan," said Diego.

"Great," said Frank. "I'll call them and book, but we may arrive quite late tomorrow. We'll take our time and stop off at a few places to get a feel for the area." His foot nudged mine. "Now, do tell us all about your farming plans."

12

"No, not the motorway," Frank said the next morning when Diego was about to join it just past the charming town of San Vicente de la Barquera which I'd have loved to visit.

"But it's only for a few miles," Diego said. "And it's just an hour that way."

"Straight across here," Frank ordered. "I've devised a picturesque route that'll take us through some lovely vill... countryside. The campsite's in Asturias, but we haven't seen inland Cantabria yet."

"Fair enough. I suppose we oughtn't to miss it," I said, but ten minutes later when he told Diego to turn into a nondescript hamlet called Gandarilla I protested that it didn't look up to much.

"Justin, we're here to explore, not just whizz past everywhere." We climbed out and he switched on his phone. "Now, there was a little something I wanted to show you. Ooh, I'll just ask that peasant woman if she knows where it is."

The strapping peasant woman, who looked and sounded Scandinavian to me, gave him directions and we soon reached a large, weed-infested shell of a house.

"What do you think then?" Frank asked me.

I looked at Diego.

"It must have been a fine house once," he said. "Does it have some kind of importance?"

Frank grinned. "Yes, it's the very first house that we've ever viewed together."

I didn't groan, because I knew I had to be strong. "Well, that's easy enough." I put my head through an absent window. "There, I've viewed it."

"This one's on sale for fifty grand. It's dear here, you see, being so near the coast, but as we drive into the hills you'll find that the prices gradually fall. I wanted to show you this one so you'll see how cheap some of the others are, relatively speaking, and who needs to be so near the coast anyway?"

Diego had walked through the open doorway and appeared at the window. "This is a project, not a house."

"Er, how long did you spend researching last night, Frank?" I said.

"Oh, a while." He yawned. "I made a few notes."

"Frank, I don't mind seeing some villages, but I don't want to spend the day viewing houses. I'm a long way from deciding what I want to do, so you're wasting your time if you think you're going to pressure me into buying something."

He tipped back his head and sighted me along the ridge of his nose. "And who says I necessarily want *you* to share a house with me, eh? We're not all paupers with a mere ninety grand in the bank, you know. I can easily afford to spend fifty and still have plenty left."

A little boy with blond hair, blue eyes and sun cream smeared on his nose scampered past.

"I don't think you'll get many English classes here though, Frank," said Diego. "I think most of them might know it already."

"Hmm, yes, the Viking hordes seem to have singled out this place. There are posh houses for sale for two and three hundred thousand here, but it's not for us anyway."

I was still pondering on his haughty outburst. I envisioned him living in a village in the Cantabrian hills in his house, owned by him and him alone. I imagined visiting him. The joy, well, warmth of our meeting after some time apart, a week or two with my old pal, then packing and leaving until the next time. I even pictured him standing on his doorstep, waving goodbye.

"At least this one's stopped scowling," he said to Diego.

I smiled. "Come on, let's get a move on. How many places do you plan to see?"

"Oh, there are about thirty villages and hamlets on our route, but I've only seen suitable houses in about a dozen of them."

"What time did you get to sleep last night?" Diego said.

"At about five. I fear a nasty phone bill, but one must seize the day."

We continued along the narrow, sinuous road and soon dropped into a gorgeous green valley which we were to follow south for forty-odd kilometres. It was a truly beautiful area and not quite like anywhere in Britain that I'd visited, possibly due to the absence of drystone walls. Of the twenty or so mostly tiny places on this part of the route, Frank only insisted on stopping at about half of them, such as Tudanca, a lovely hamlet with several *casas montañesas*, those houses with the wooden balconies. There we viewed a ruin similar to the one at Gandarilla, but at a third of the price, and a house with a roof, of sorts, for €36,000.

"The trouble is, someone takes a place like this, does it up, and suddenly it's worth a hundred grand more," Frank said.

"This is a desirable area and not so far from the coast," I said. "You'll get no bargains here."

"And in winter you'd be lonely," said Diego. "I bet a lot of the posher houses are holiday homes, and we've seen the odd rural hotel too."

"It's lovely here, but out of your price range, Frank. It's a really touristy area. We've already spied the Picos de Europa and we're only going to get nearer to them now, I hope."

He smiled. "Yes, we start to head west soon." He looked at his phone. "Next stop Pesaguero, where I hope to show you that rural Cantabria isn't out of our reach."

"Out of your reach. Drive on, Diego."

Pesaguero was much the same as the other hamlets, consisting of about twenty houses in varying states of repair.

"Where the hell do people go shopping or get a drink around here?" said Diego as we strolled along the roughly asphalted street. "We've seen nothing for ages."

"From here they'll go to Potes, a mere ten miles away. Ha, there it is! Feast your eyes on that little dream home."

Little it certainly was, being a modest bungalow, but all the roof tiles appeared to be in place and the door and window frames had been painted green some time in the last twenty or thirty years.

Frank scrolled down. "This one doesn't need much doing to it; nothing we couldn't manage, Justin."

"I'll give you a hand when I come on holiday."

"And it's only sixty-five grand, which means sixty, or fifty-five once I've got to work on them. So, Justin, you see there are places within our price range after all."

As I took a couple of photos on my phone I felt him literally breathing down my neck. I swore I could hear his heart beating too.

"Ah, just imagine living in this beautiful spot, Justin. Nestled in the bosom of nature and able to pop into Potes whenever we want a bit of company. Ooh, look, there's a number on the sign. I'll ring it and see if anyone's got the key."

"Frank, I've only taken the photos so I can show them to you when you've sobered up. It's a tiny house in a tiny hamlet where

I'm guessing hardly anyone lives in winter. You'd end up going crazy alone here. Instead of popping into Potes, why don't you look for a house there?"

"Bah, Potes is jam-packed with hotels and restaurants. All right to visit, but not to live in. We need to find a normal sort of place."

"I must say I'm surprised at the number of posh houses we've seen," said Diego. "Cantabria and Asturias aren't that big really, and it looks like well-off Spaniards and foreigners have already decided they're good places to have a house. If it weren't for them, all these hamlets would be dying like those in Soria. You're not going to see any real, untouristy villages until we leave the Picos, so if I were you I'd forget about houses for now."

Here, here, I thought, but he hadn't done yet.

"When we head down towards Astorga we'll start to leave the tourist trail and I think we'll see more normal villages. I reckon that'll be a better place to start house hunting, Frank. All the hamlets we've seen look lovely today, but if we'd done the route on a wet winter's day it'd have seemed grim and desolate, and I know it can rain for days on end up here, so you really want somewhere with places to hang out and chat to folk."

Frank grunted.

"I'm glad we came this way though," I said. "It's been a lovely drive."

He sighed. "Yes, and I suppose one must know one's limits. I should thank my lucky stars that my dad left me all that cash and that I've given up drinking. I shan't pester you about houses again."

"OK."

"Until we leave the Picos. Diego, you haven't told us who we're going to visit in Astorga yet."

He smiled. "It's a surprise; a nice one, I think. Let's get some lunch in Potes."

After pottering around the pleasant streets of Potes we had lunch in a bar with lots of other tourists, before cruising north on a better road through even more mountainous terrain. After descending a long pass through a rocky ravine, the road marked the border between Cantabria and Asturias for a few miles, after which we headed west through a wooded valley and glimpsed the majestic Picos to the south. Frank didn't order Diego to stop at any of the villages we saw, probably because they were so obviously tourist magnets, like Arenas de Cabrales, the one just past our campsite, which proved to be chock-a-block with rural hotels.

After Frank had made his usual remark about the blasted motorhomes getting all the best spots, we pitched out tents on a slightly sloping field with no shade, before heading off to find our Scottish friends, who'd been given a flat pitch beside some trees. It was still almost thirty degrees at five o'clock, so we gladly sat down in the shade on their canvas chairs and sipped iced lemon tea which Yvonne had prepared. When Craig asked us where we'd been, Frank anticipated my reply and described the route without so much as mentioning his reason for devising it, but they were both astute enough to guess.

I won't go into too much detail about the three nights we spent at that fine campsite with our new friends, because we had a pleasantly orthodox time of it. We did a couple of longish walks, paddled in the nearby river, ate some tasty meals, and generally chilled out in those beautiful surroundings. After the Comillas fiasco Frank didn't take out his camera once and spoke only in general terms about future film projects. He also kept his word not to pester me about buying a house, although his eyes lit up when Yvonne and Craig spoke of their hopes of finding a suitable smallholding further west in Galicia, where the terrain was more rolling and tourism far less intense.

On Tuesday morning we ate our last campsite breakfast for a while, before taking leave of our accommodating hosts.

"I'm sure we'll meet again before long," Frank said as he pumped Craig's hand.

"We'll certainly be back next summer, whether we've bought a place by then or not."

"I think I'll be living here in the north, though I haven't a clue where yet."

Diego kissed Yvonne. "Hopefully we can all meet up in August. I'll drive to wherever you are, and you're welcome to come to Ólvega too." He glanced at me. "And Deza, of course."

"Justin might still be working in Lancashire," said Frank. "But I suppose he may manage a fortnight's holiday."

I smiled. "We'll see."

"I'd like to come with you to Galicia now," said Frank. "But Diego's arranged a stay in Astorga, so we have to go there first."

"It has to be this week. My friend's going to Ólvega on Sunday," he said. "We can always go up to Galicia afterwards."

"Or down to Fermoselle to see your uncle," I said.

He frowned. "Yes, or there."

After waving them off we struck camp and loaded the car.

"How far is it to Astorga, Diego?" I asked.

"About 262 kilometres by the quickest route, up to the coast and then mostly motorways west and south. It should take about three hours."

Frank smiled. "But only 240 kilometres the way we're actually going, round the Picos and south into northern León, which abounds with affordable houses."

I groaned. "Here we go again."

"Indeed we do." He rubbed his hands together. "My period of reflection is over and I must resume my house search, *my* being the operative word, as I've decided to go it alone."

"I…"

He raised his hand and addressed the mountains. "Yes, there comes a time in a man's life when he must strike out into the unknown and rely on no-one but himself. While you've both proved to be good travelling companions, the parting of our ways must inevitably arrive one day soon. Diego will return to Ólvega, form a fine family, and become a pillar of the community, whereas my destiny lies south or west or maybe south-west of here, in some unsuspecting burgh where I'll make my films and… ha, who knows what the future may hold?"

I nudged Diego. "He prepared that earlier. And what about me, Frank?"

"You?" He shrugged. "You must decide for yourself. I can't be your guiding star, after all."

"That's fine by me. Now guide us along this route of yours."

"I've told Si… my friend that we'll probably be there for lunch," said Diego.

"Then tell this mystery mate to expect us later. We have an action-packed day ahead of us and I doubt we'll sight the Castilian plains for a good few hours. I'm sure four days will be plenty of time with this pal of yours anyway." He waved at the Picos. "Farewell until next time, when I'll conquer your peaks instead of strolling around in your valleys." He hopped into the passenger seat and shut the door.

"I think he's recharged his batteries," said Diego.

"I'm afraid so."

The valley became wider as we trundled west to Cangas de Onís in a convoy of cars, and after crawling through the pretty town where I wouldn't have minded lingering, we took the road south through yet more spectacular scenery. We saw several hamlets similar to those of our Cantabrian tour, but it wasn't until we'd passed through a stunning gorge into the province of León that Frank took out his phone.

"Au revoir, Asturias," he said, before beginning to swipe and prod with a vengeance.

"It's still very green and mountainous," I said a few miles later.

"Yes, we're not quite out of the tourist woods yet. Oseja de Sajambre is up ahead, riddled with rural hotels, then a squiggle of a road which will no doubt take us up onto the Castilian plateau, where men are men and a house can be had for a song."

After ascending an endless pass the terrain became less abrupt and trees much scarcer. A huge reservoir soon came into view and Frank announced that we were about to visit the singular village of Nuevo Riaño.

"The mountains across the reservoir are great, and so is that bridge," I said once we'd arrived. "But this place looks really new."

He passed me his phone. "Here's a photo of it."

"It looks old here. Where are these streets?"

He chuckled. "Underwater. Because of the reservoir they moved everyone out of Riaño and a few more villages in the eighties and built this place for them. If Spain had joined Europe earlier it wouldn't have happened, as that sort of thing was banned shortly afterwards."

Diego sighed. "I guess they need a lot of water south of here, because they're not short of it to the north."

Frank smiled. "Yes, and south of here is where I may find my new home."

I looked around. "So are you not thinking of buying one of these flats?"

"I could, because they go for fifty grand, but I don't think so somehow."

We had coffee in a new bar full of old men, before driving across the extremely long reservoir bridge and into Frank's supposed promised land. After bypassing a few hamlets we reached the small town of Cistierna, flanked by a hemisphere of hills to the north and rolling countryside to the south, and where, Frank declared, he'd be spoilt for choice.

"There are at least half a dozen decent houses here for less than sixty thousand. I suggest we have a wander round and try to spot them, then I'll treat you to lunch so I can meet the locals."

"Oh, all right," I said.

"Quite frankly, Frank, I think you're mad," said Diego.

I laughed. "Have you only just realised?"

"Well, I've always known he's not quite as sane as we are, but it's just struck me how crazy this house buying business is. I mean, you wouldn't know a single soul here, Frank. Who on earth goes and buys a house somewhere for no reason?"

Frank just smiled indulgently.

"But he's had this on his mind for a while now, Diego, so why the sudden flash of insight?"

"Because here he's got me worried. In those tiny hamlets I knew he wouldn't be daft enough to buy a place, but this is a town. It's full of people. Frank likes people and it'll only take one or two of them to be nice to him and he might start signing things. I... I think we should clear out and go to Silvia's before it's too late."

Frank's eyebrows rose. "Silvia's?"

"In Astorga." He sighed. "She's my sister's best mate from school, but we've always been good friends too. She got married to a guy from there, but they divorced last year, so now it's just her and her son Rubén, who must be about twelve now. She's lovely, so I wanted it to be a surprise, but, well…"

"You thought a timely distraction was in order," I said.

"Exactly."

"And I await our meeting with bated breath, Diego, but I still want to stroll around here. It's nearly time for lunch anyway, so let's go."

Cistierna was an unremarkable sort of place without any tourists to speak of, despite its lovely surroundings, so I suppose most of them headed north to the reservoir and beyond. Frank only traced one of the houses on his list and although it seemed to be in good repair, it was situated on a busy road. We adjourned to a restaurant for lunch and found the food good and the people politely curious. I quite liked the compact little town, but wouldn't have dreamed of buying a house there, in case I ended up not making friends. Over coffee I reminded Frank that his original idea had been to rent a house.

"Yes, that's occurred to me too. The house-buying bug hit me so hard that I forgot about that eminently sensible option." He switched on his phone and I glanced at Diego.

He winked. "Yes, Silvia will be looking forward to seeing us. She feels rather lonely in Astorga now and comes home to Ólvega whenever she can. She thinks she ought to stay there so that her son can be near his father, but she only has a couple of close friends."

"Uh-huh," Frank murmured absently as he viewed his screen, so I urged Diego on.

"She's getting fed up of the men there too. They assume she's looking for another partner, and being such an attractive woman they're always asking her out, when all she wants is to be left alone." I shook my head. "For now, that is, and by them, because she wouldn't get together with another Astorga man." Frank glanced up. "Astorga's quite an insular place, you see, and after fourteen years she's had enough of it."

"How old did you say she was?" Frank asked.

"I didn't, but she went to school with my sister, so she'll be about thirty-seven."

I rubbed my hands together. "Well, I'd like to meet her right away."

Frank sighed and pocketed his phone. "Yes, I suppose we should be going. I've only found flats and one huge house for rent anyway."

On the road to León, Frank felt it was his duty to utter a few words of caution.

"I noticed you prick up your ears when Diego said that his friend Silvia was attractive, Justin, but I strongly advise you not to pester her."

My mouth fell open, but as I was in the back as usual, he couldn't see it. "Me?"

"Yes, you don't know Spanish women like I do, you see. Although they're fond of being flattered, I've always found it best to let them take the lead, so please bear that in mind."

"I will, Frank, thanks."

"Did you have any serious girlfriends when you were in Spain?" Diego asked him.

He chuckled. "I had plenty of girlfriends, but none of them lasted long. They all wanted to reform me and I wasn't ready for that, so I just moved on to the next one. Ah, yes, I sowed a few wild oats in Madrid and Seville all right."

"And Almería?"

"Less so there, I'm afraid, because while Spanish girls don't mind a man being a little drunk at the end of the night, they don't like it if he's half-cut when he meets them."

"Half-cut?"

"Pissed," I said. Frank had related tales to me about his many brief liaisons, but he'd also told me about a couple of more long-lasting relationships. In Blackburn and sober once more, he'd complained that his 'mojo' didn't work for him there and that Englishwomen only became receptive after a few drinks, whereas Spanish women tended to make it clear if they liked a man without first resorting to stimulants. I already had an inkling that this was true, because I'd noticed a couple of ladies eyeing me candidly during our travels, something that rarely occurred in Blackburn before ten in the evening, in a pub.

Not far from Cistierna we found ourselves on the plains once more, and after joining a dual-carriageway we skirted the city of León and whizzed west past endless fields until the twin spires of Astorga's cathedral came into view.

"Astorga's supposed to be a really historic place," I said as we passed an unfinished block of flats. "So why are the outskirts just as scruffy as most other towns we've seen?"

"That's progress," said Diego. "Though I can't see much of it here."

"No wonderful industrial estate like in Ólvega then?" said Frank.

"I doubt it," he said, missing or pretending to miss Frank's jibe. "Most people probably have crap jobs in hotels and restaurants. Astorga's on the Santiago pilgrim trail, so Silvia says it's full of tourists most of the year." He turned up the volume on the sat-nav. "Let's see where she lives."

Silvia lived in a modern second-floor flat on the outskirts which she and her ex had bought new some years earlier. She worked in a chemist's shop, but said she could take some time off to show us around. She regretted that one of us would have to sleep on the sofa, as there was only one spare room with twin beds. She was affectionate towards Diego in a sisterly sort of way and didn't seem to mind that he had two older friends in tow. She was also tall, slim and so pretty that even Frank had been left speechless, but not for long, as the scheming devil soon volunteered to sleep on the sofa.

"I've had the single tent for the last few nights, so I'll let these two have the beds," he said in Spanish, his eyes sparkling so brightly that one might have imagined he had a switch somewhere.

"All right," she said, lowering her eyes to avoid the dazzle, as most of his undeservedly white teeth were also on display. "What did you think of Ólvega?"

"It's a nice town," I said.

"It's a *wonderful* place," Frank gushed. "I love the way it's managed to harmonise its historical past with its dynamic industrial present, and future, of course, ha ha!"

Her silky-smooth brow creased and she glanced at Diego, as if to ask him who this flattering fool was. Fortunately for me I was too gobsmacked by her beauty to say much. Though thirty-seven, she didn't look a day over thirty. Her long dark hair was so glossy, her facial and bodily features so well-proportioned, her brown eyes so luminous, and her voice so soft that an inane smile and a mumbled 'gracias' was all I could manage when she'd shown us around the flat, given us towels, and left us to freshen up.

"What do you think of Silvia then?" Diego said with a grin.

"She's very pleasant," I said.

Frank chuckled. "Justin's smitten already. He was following her around like a… lascivious lapdog."

"She was leading the way. Er, don't forget that she's Diego's and his sister's friend, Frank, not some floozy to be ogled and buttered up."

Diego's eyes opened wide. "Buttered up? I don't like the sound of that."

"It means flattered," I said.

"Both of you remember that she has a child too. He's staying with his grandparents in the country right now."

"I love kids," said Frank. "Still, although Silvia's very nice and all that, I think a couple of days here will suffice to see the sights, then we'll toddle off somewhere else."

"Suits me," I said, as I feared I might find Silvia's presence a little too stimulating and make a fool of myself. For a man in his mid-forties who hadn't had much luck with women for a while, it was quite disturbing to be thrown into close proximity with such a pretty and agreeable single lady, so I warned myself to behave like a perfect gentleman at all times. I didn't fancy my chances much, but I resolved to be pleasant and polite and to look out for any signs of attraction. Only then might I… well, I didn't quite know what I'd do, but as she was going to Ólvega on holiday soon, I guessed I'd be eager to return there before long.

Frank sniggered. "Justin's already plotting how to woo her."

"I'm more worried about you than Justin, Frank. I *know* you offered to take the sofa in the hope of being alone with her late at night, but I fear that you'll only behave foolishly. My sister told me that at least two wealthy local men have asked her out and she turned them both down. Her marriage didn't work out and she's determined not to get involved with anyone until she's fairly sure that he's right for her."

Frank tutted. "I'm not a fool, Diego, and I certainly won't be making the first move."

I spluttered.

"And you don't even speak decent Spanish, so you've no bloody chance." He smiled at Diego. "Ha, you don't happen to have designs on her yourself, do you?"

He pulled a face. "But she's older than me, Frank."

"Only by about three years."

He shook his head. "No, I do find her attractive, but that's unthinkable. Besides, I wouldn't want my future wife to have had children by anyone else."

"Will she have to be a virgin?" Frank asked.

"Well, that's asking a lot these days, but I would like that, yes. Not so many years ago it would have been a requirement, but I've got to be realistic. I'm off for a shower."

Sitting face to face on the beds, Frank and I silently weighed each other up for a few moments, then I asked him if he was now in favour of renting a house again.

He shrugged. "I suppose so. It makes more sense. I think I got the buying bug because I've never owned my own place before."

"Hmm, that's true. It's not all it's cracked up to be, you know. It's a lot of fuss and if you make the wrong choice you have to sell the damned thing. I've realised that a lot of rented houses in Spain come furnished."

He grinned. "I could have told you that. So have you been swotting up on the subject?"

"A bit. I've looked into this online work business too and I'm sure I could get some. Maybe not a lot, but enough to cover my basic costs, touch wood." I tapped the headboard.

"Hmm, the only serious string to my work bow is English teaching, I'm afraid, so I'll have to go somewhere at least as big as Cistierna, or here."

I smiled. "How about Ólvega? It isn't so big, but there must be plenty of money around for luxuries like English classes."

He wrinkled his nose. "Oh, Ólvega, it's… well, it's not the sort of place I imagined living in."

I pointed out that quaint places tended to attract tourists. "What do you prefer, hordes of trippers or hard-working locals?"

"Neither, really, but I should know not to idealise Spain by now."

I told him that after thinking long and hard about it, I'd decided that Ólvega would be my best starting point in Spain. This wasn't strictly true, as only in Cistierna had it struck me how absurd it would be to go to a place where I didn't know anyone. I also reasoned that if Frank ended up sharing with me, I'd rather be in Diego's town than stuck with him as my guide and mentor elsewhere. In Ólvega, with Diego's help, I'd soon get to know some non-English speakers with whom to practise my Spanish without having Frank breathing down my neck all the time. On the whole it seemed by far the least risky option, and I could always move on when I'd learnt the language. After Frank had sat staring at my feet for a while, I asked him what he thought.

"I'm still thinking."

"Being in Ólvega would help to ease me into Spanish life, but of course you're an old hand already."

"Yes, I am. Hmm, I think drinking always helped me to make friends in a new place, as I didn't bother with the folk in the language schools much. In Cistierna today I did have a moment of weakness, I must say."

"What kind?"

"Well, in a small town like that you either hit it off with folk or you don't. My, er… gregarious nature might be my passport to friendship, but then again if I rubbed someone up the wrong way they might spread the word that I'm a pest and turn folk against me. I'll have to sleep on this Ólvega idea though. It'll seem like chickening out in a way, but if we're renting we'll only need to give a month's notice and we can be off somewhere else. I certainly don't fancy another winter in Darwen."

We were plunged in thought once more when Diego returned in his boxer shorts.

"Ah, a clean shower for once. I… oh, have you been fighting over Silvia already?"

"Who?" said Frank. "Oh, Silvia, no, we've been talking about maybe renting a place in Ólvega for a while."

His right eyelid twitched, but he managed a smile. "Well, I guess you wouldn't be my responsibility, Frank. Are you sure you made it up with Revilla though?"

"Revilla? Ha, if we bump into him you'll see how he remembers me."

"I bet he will."

"Maybe I'll set up a film school there."

"Frank, you need to *go* to a film school, not set one up," I said.

"Well, you know what I mean, get people taking part in projects. Hmm, yes, I'm beginning to come round to this idea of yours, Justin. I'll have my shower now."

I confessed to Diego that I'd as good as proposed a flat-sharing scheme in Ólvega and explained why. As he dressed a pregnant pause ensued, but he finally said that on the whole he'd be glad to have us.

"You've always been welcome to come, of course, and Frank hasn't put his foot in it for a while now, so maybe he's learnt from his mistakes."

I tapped the headboard again. "Let's hope so."

13

While in the shower I imagined that the third of our tête-à-têtes would also revolve around the subject of Ólvega, but when we walked into town a while later Diego expressed concern that Frank was about to vex Silvia.

"When you went for a shower he started quizzing me about her and I tried to put him off. I told him I doubted he was her type, as she's quite a conventional person, even a little boring sometimes, but look at him now, jabbing away into her ear."

"Jabbering."

"Jabbering, yes, about Ólvega by the sound of it. I wonder why."

I chuckled. "He may be planning ahead. Do you think she'll go back to live there anytime soon?"

"I'm not sure. I know she wants to. Maybe we'll find out while we're here."

"If Frank ever leaves her alone."

Astorga is an atmospheric place at twilight and we strolled past the immense Gothic cathedral and the episcopal palace designed by none other than Gaudí, before taking a look at the imposing Roman walls. We agreed to do a proper tour the following day and visit the Roman museum.

"There's also a chocolate museum," Silvia said at a cafe in the splendid old square. She'd told us little about the cathedral, palace and other fine buildings, possibly due to Frank prattling away most of the time, or maybe because she'd become bored of seeing them. About halfway through our dinner of tapas Frank declared that he'd be taking his film camera out the next day in the hope of finding someone interesting to interview. I was all for it, as it would allow Silvia to see another facet of his character, that of the meddlesome man with a movie camera, and I didn't think she'd be impressed.

Frank beamed at her. "I'd really like to interview you too, Silvia, if you don't mind."

She smiled sweetly. "No, Frank, I don't wish to be interviewed. I don't like being filmed and I don't have anything interesting to say," she said so firmly that even he knew it would be useless to insist.

This rejection must have knocked the wind out of his sails, because he began to eat silently and survey the passing tourists. This was my chance to ingratiate myself with our enchanting hostess, but I soon found that her enchantment worked mostly on the eyes, because try as I might I couldn't make her utter more than polite replies to my open-ended enquiries. By coffee time Diego had begun to talk about the only thing that appeared to interest her, Ólvega. As they chattered about the people and places they knew, her eyes shone once more and I realised that she was just a small town girl who'd made the mistake of getting hitched to a chap from elsewhere. She said she hoped to sell her flat and return home the following year, because her son would be starting secondary school, so the separation from his friends would be slightly less painful. Young Rubén had visited Ólvega every summer, so he already had pals there and she felt sure he'd soon like it better, because Olvegueños were so much more open and friendly than the Astorganos, who tended to be clannish and set in their ways.

At this point in her unusually fluid discourse Frank performed a mighty yawn. I say performed, because he stretched out his arms and tipped back his head to illustrate the extent of his fatigue.

"Oh, excuse me, but I'm *so* sleepy. It's been such a long day," said the man who'd got up at a quarter to nine.

Silvia seemed unperturbed, even pleased, by his rudeness, as it surely signalled the end of his verbal onslaught. On the way back she told us that she'd have to work the next day after all, as a large consignment of medicines was due to arrive and she'd have to open all the boxes, catalogue the new stock, and rearrange the display. It was an unnecessarily detailed explanation and when we'd retired for the night I told Diego that I didn't quite believe her.

"No, I don't think she fancied spending all day wandering around with us. I've only ever seen her in Ólvega, and she's always happy and chatty there." He chuckled. "I think Frank's got the message now."

"Yes… yes, and I'm getting to know her a bit. I think I was blinded by her beauty at first, but she's just a… well, a regular gal really."

"She's not especially bright, if that's what you mean."

"No, well, not especially, but–"

"Ah, if she were ten years younger she'd be perfect for me. Who wants a clever wife anyway? A wife should be a faithful partner and a good mother. I think she's been both of those things, and she's beautiful too, so one shouldn't ask for more."

I thought about my intelligent ex-wife and her total lack of interest in anything more cultural than *Antiques Roadshow*. "I want to meet a more well-rounded companion really. Someone who reads books and has interests and doesn't want to watch TV every single evening."

"Yes, with Emma it was either TV or going out to the pubs. I never really got used to that. In Ólvega – well, in most of Spain – people are out and about, strolling and chatting and having the odd drink, not at home watching TV or out getting pissed." He shook his head on the pillow. "I don't know how I stood it for so long now. I might write a book about it. I'll call it *The Lost Years* and it'll be about five pages long. At least I met you, I suppose."

"And Frank."

"Yes, and Frank." He yawned and switched off his bedside light.

I left mine on. "Will we be going to see your uncle next then?"

He sighed. "Oh, I suppose so. If I don't go I'll feel guilty later, and Fermoselle sounds like quite a curious place."

"So have you never been?"

"No, and no-one's seen him since he ra… went there, or only briefly. I wrote to him a few years later and we spoke on the phone a few times when I was in Blackburn. I was young when he went away, so I didn't feel angry like the others, even my sister, who must have been about fifteen then."

"Are you going to tell me… well, anything about him?"

"No, and not to surprise you like I did with Silvia, but so you don't judge him because of his past."

"Fair enough. You'd better call him first."

"I already did, a couple of days ago. When I said we might go he was delighted, so we'll have to now. I only hope he's… oh, I don't know what I hope. Goodnight, Justin."

I switched off my light. "Buenas noches."

After our initial hiccups the next two days in Astorga went smoothly enough, despite Frank toting his video camera everywhere with him. On Wednesday afternoon he interviewed a Chilean couple who were on the pilgrim trail to Santiago, but he refrained from challenging their religious beliefs, probably because they'd sworn to do the pilgrimage if their child recovered from a serious illness, which she had. On Thursday morning he collared two local youngsters near Gaudí's palace and asked them what they liked and disliked about their home town. Both lads couldn't wait to go to León or further afield to study and intended to end up living in a city, because Astorga was deadly dull and mucked up with tourists. In the afternoon he left the camera in the flat, because Silvia had taken a few hours off work and expressly forbade him from bringing it along.

She took us to the chocolate museum, where we learnt that in 1520 the famous conquistador Hernán Cortés had first brought the stuff back from America, where the Aztecs and Mayas had been scoffing it for centuries. His daughter later married the Marquis of Astorga, which is probably why the town became one of the leading Spanish manufacturers during the following centuries. Although it wasn't the most riveting museum I'd ever visited, Silvia seemed to think it the high spot of a town founded two millennia ago, but there's no accounting for historical tastes and she is fond of chocolate.

On a cafe terrace in the modern part of town Diego finally told her that we were thinking of going to live in Ólvega. As Frank had been behaving himself and my conduct had been nothing short of exemplary, she seemed pleased by our provisional choice and spoke of the town in such glowing terms that Astorga seemed like a trifling backwater in comparison. We told her how we intended to earn our daily bread and Frank also mentioned his plans to set up some sort of film-making initiative, upon which she set him atremble again by saying that her son might be interested and that she herself wouldn't be averse to becoming involved in something of that nature.

Frank wiped a dribble of olive oil from his chin. "But you didn't even want to give me an interview, Silvia."

She shrugged. "Not here, no. At home I feel much more relaxed. If Rubén takes an interest I may come along too, but not until next year, of course. Ah, I can't wait to leave this place. I suppose I'm paranoid that everyone's wondering what I'm going to do, but when I put the flat up for sale they'll know."

"In Ólvega everyone will wonder what you're going to do too, Silvia," said Diego.

She smiled. "I won't mind there. Here it's none of their business."

For a moment I feared that Frank was going to renew his wooing, but the man of many conquests chose to remain strong and almost silent for the rest of the evening, no doubt hoping to leave her with a good overall impression. Later when Diego and I had retired to our room we did hear the murmur of conversation for a while, but during the following days Frank remained smilingly mute on the subject of their little parley, so I was almost sure that nothing of importance had been discussed.

14

He was in an unusually good mood the next morning though, as Diego drove us the roughly 183 kilometres due south to Fermoselle, a remote place just a stone's throw from the Portuguese border. We traversed endless plains during most of the two hour, 4.8 litres/100 kilometre journey, and only after crossing the tip of a huge reservoir did we begin to discern more greenery, before spotting the large village perched nobly on the hillside. The River Duero – the Douro from the Portuguese side – marks the frontier and the abrupt valley forms a sort of narrow oasis for many miles. We found this out later, of course, because on our arrival Diego first had to prepare us for our meeting with Uncle Abelardo. It had begun to rain, so we'd parked up and hurried into a bar in the small but elegant main square.

"I might go to see him alone first. I haven't seen him for over twenty years. He sent me a photo some time ago, otherwise I doubt I'd recognise him."

"Is he gay?" said Frank.

"What sort of question is that?" I snapped.

"A straight one. Justin, the Spaniards are notorious homophobes, so if he's fallen into disgrace I'm guessing that might be why."

Diego sighed. "He's right, Justin, but his disgrace isn't because of being gay." He glanced around at the few elderly customers. "He came out when he was at university in Zaragoza, so the family had got used to it by the time the... episode happened, when he was thirty-two, I think. Even my dad had got his head around it, my mum told me later. He was really proud when his little brother went off to study, as no-one in the family had done that before, so when he came out it was a shock, as my dad's quite macho and had to put up with a lot of joking around from the other blokes at work. Anyway, Uncle Abelardo became a teacher and got a job in Soria, so he came home quite often. He never spoke about his love life and didn't seem especially gay." He chuckled. "My dad even hoped that he'd somehow recover from his 'condition' and get married – to a woman, I mean – then the shit hit the fan and his name's been mud ever since."

"Your grasp of colloquial English is excellent, Diego," said Frank.

"Justin's to thank for most of it. A lot of folk in Blackburn carried on speaking to me as if I were a halfwit even after I became quite fluent."

"That's just the way some of them talk."

"Er, so what happened?" I said.

Diego sighed. "Oh, I hope this won't turn you against him before you even meet him."

Frank sniggered. "I think you underestimate our broad-mindedness, Diego."

"Yes, we're not so easily shocked," I said.

"We're men of the world," Frank said. "Especially me."

Diego sipped his beer, cleared his throat, and looked around again. "Right, here goes. He... he ran off with a pupil."

"What!" Frank cried. "The bastard!" He slid back his chair with a screech and jumped to his feet. "Right, drink up. We're out of here." He shook his finger at Diego. "How could you bring us to see such a monster? Oh, what a wasted journey! We could have been in Galicia by now, instead of in this den of bumpkins and perverts."

"I meant ex-pupil. The lad was nineteen."

"Sit down, Frank. You're making an exhibition of yourself."

"Not yet." He shuffled around like a constipated bear.

"He swore to me on the phone years ago that nothing had happened while the lad was at school. A couple of years later he bumped into him in a pub where gay blokes hung out and they started seeing each other. My uncle tried to keep it secret, but Soria's a small city and the director of the school found out and assumed it had been going on for a long time. My uncle was suspended while they investigated and I think he flipped a bit. They took off for Portugal, but didn't get any further than here."

Frank sat down. "And are they still together?"

"No, after a few days the lad emptied my uncle's wallet and went home."

Frank stood up. "Yes, on realising that his evil teacher had corrupted him."

"Estáte quieto!" barked an old man who was trying to concentrate on his game of dominoes.

He sat down.

Diego smiled. "Look, Frank, my uncle told me that the lad knew perfectly well what he was doing. He was a cruel sort of person, in fact, and my uncle was worried that if he was asked to attend some sort of enquiry at the school he'd make up all sorts of things, just out of spite. That's why he decided to stay here for a while."

"For over twenty years," I said.

"He did go back to meet the director and some school officials, but there was so much suspicion and bad feeling that he resigned and moved here permanently."

"Yes, to corrupt the local youth," Frank muttered.

"Evidently not, because he's still here and gets on fine with everyone. From what I've gathered he never met the partner he hoped to find and now prefers to be single."

"Why hasn't he managed to make it up with his family?" I asked him. "From what you've told us he didn't really behave badly, just a bit impulsively."

Diego shrugged. "I think it's partly down to pride. He wrote to them at first, but when he didn't get the sort of replies he expected he thought, to hell with them. At his mother's funeral he came and stood at the back of the church, but when the service was over he'd gone. My dad went to both hotels but he wasn't in either. He was seen early the next day at the cemetery, so they assumed he'd stayed somewhere out of town. Pride, you see."

"Where were you?" I asked.

"I'd just gone to Blackburn. I should have flown home, but I was worried that I'd lose my crappy job at the warehouse, so I didn't. I still regret that. I'd have gone to join him in the church and things might have turned out differently."

"And his dad's funeral?"

"He didn't go, or at least no-one saw him. He'd been much closer to his mother."

"How did he find out about her funeral?"

He shrugged. "Someone must have called him."

"Is this a full-scale investigation, Justin?" said Frank.

"I'm just curious."

Diego smiled. "I'm glad he asked, and I think I'm glad I've told you the story, otherwise it might have come out bit by bit and spoilt our stay. I'm not sure my uncle will want you to know all this, so keep it to yourselves for the time being. Try to erase it from your minds and just take him as he is."

"Fat chance of that with this one around," I said. "I fear it'll be a short stay that might not end well."

"In that case I'll get you a hotel room for the night and see him alone, then we'll go in the morning. I'm not leaving here without spending some time with him."

Frank's sigh was so loud and long that both domino players turned to glare at him.

He held up his hands. "Perdónenme, señores." He smiled sadly at Diego. "Diego," he purred. "My initial shock was caused by you mistakenly saying that the lad was his pupil. If you'd just told us he was a consenting adult of nineteen I wouldn't have batted an eyelid. I've known many gay blokes in Spain – not intimately, of course – and I consider myself one of the most tolerant people I know, something that can't be said for many of your compatriots, who're about as PC as Bernard Manning."

"Who's he?"

"He was a sexist, racist comedian whose Indian neighbours said was a very nice man in real life," I said. "In fact I think I'd rather go to see your uncle with him than with Frank." I had a sly idea. "Look, why don't we do what you suggested? Frank and me can knock around here and see the sights, then we'll shoot off tomorrow."

"Well…"

"Nonsense, we'll all go." Frank finished his coffee. "In fact that's quite enough pussyfooting around for one day." He stood up. "Diego, lead me to your uncle."

I chuckled. "Sit down, Frank." He complied. "Before we go you must solemnly swear on… something that you'll do your very best not to put your foot in it. Remember this is a really significant meeting for Diego, so if you spoil it for him I'll never forgive you, and I mean that."

Frank opened his bag and took out his video camera.

"Oh, no," Diego moaned.

"Justin, please take this, and if I don't prove to be the most polite, considerate and enlightened guest you've ever seen, you can throw it off the nearest cliff."

"Put it back in the bag, Frank. I'll know where to find it."

We went up to the bar and Diego asked the man where Abelardo lived.

"The artist?"

"Yes."

He accompanied us to the door and indicated a narrow street. "About two hundred metres along there, on the left."

"Gracias," said Diego.

"Gracias," I said.

"Do you know him?" said Frank.

The portly man looked puzzled. "Of course. He's lived here for years."

"I don't suppose he gets many visitors."

"Abelardo? More than anyone else here. People come from Madrid and Barcelona to see him."

"What kin–"

I yanked him out. "Hasta luego," I said, and to Diego in English. "We'd better find a hotel after all. He's a hopeless case."

"I was about to ask what kind of art he did," Frank whined.

"Bullshit."

"Oh, come on," said Diego. "He knows you're here anyway. We can always find Frank a room later."

"You didn't say he was an artist," said Frank.

"I thought it was just a hobby."

Uncle Abelardo's three-storey house had a neat ochre facade, matte green window shutters and a huge door with a brass knocker in the shape of a fish. Diego rapped it and a slim man of medium height with unkempt grey hair soon appeared. He wore round glasses, a checked short-sleeved shirt, blue jeans, leather sandals, and a welcoming smile on his lean, handsome face. He resembled his nephew a lot and as the two men hugged I saw that Frank was weighing him up. Diego introduced us and he shook our hands firmly before leading us inside out of the drizzle. He ushered us into a spartan sitting room furnished with upright armchairs around a big stone fireplace. The one small picture on the wall opposite bore the signature of Domínguez and the rest of the lemon-coloured walls were bare.

"So you are Diego's good friend from England, Justin," he said in fluent English as I admired the abstract picture.

"Yes."

"And Frank here is another good friend, though more recent," Diego said in Spanish.

He smiled at Frank. "Yes, of course, he mentioned you the last time we spoke," he replied in Spanish, and never spoke in English again, setting a sterling example to my linguistically feckless friends.

"Lunch will be ready in a little while, so we'll have a drink in here first. Is beer all right for you?"

"Sin alcohol para mí, por favor," said Frank.

He smiled. "Para mí también. I haven't drunk alcohol for years. Excuse me a moment."

He left and we instinctively looked at Frank.

"I like him," he said, and believe it or not our fears of a major clanger ended provisionally within the next ten minutes and definitively over lunch.

Abelardo asked us about our trip and we summarised our travels until a smiling, middle-aged lady popped her head around the door and announced that lunch was ready. He introduced us to María, who came in to clean and cook in the mornings, before leading us through to an equally spartan dining room with a big old table and six chairs, a few bookshelves, no television or other devices, and no paintings on the walls. We ate salad, garlic soup, *Arroz a la zamorana* – rice with meat and vegetables – and fruit for dessert. Abelardo continued to enquire about our lives and say nothing about himself until, over coffee, he asked us if Diego had mentioned the reason for him coming to Fermoselle. We nodded, he chuckled and shook his head, and any remaining shards of social ice were finally dissolved. Frank's reaction to Diego's revelation had been typical histrionics on his part, of course, but it was still a relief when his respectful demeanour assured us that he meant to behave himself.

"So you're an artist, Abelardo," Frank said as he glanced at the walls.

He chuckled. "Yes, but down here I prefer to disconnect from my work. I'll show you my studio presently."

I asked him about the picture in the sitting room and he said it was a gift from a grateful client from Barcelona; a wealthy one, I realised later when I looked up Óscar Domínguez (1906-1957) and found that some of his paintings had sold for tens of thousands of dollars, but Abelardo was far too discreet to boast about such a valuable acquisition. When Diego told him that we were thinking of going to live in Ólvega he smiled and said that we could do worse.

"I intend to go one day soon. My own stubbornness has prevented me from going for a long time. I hope Diego's visit will pave the way for an enjoyable trip," he said with great equanimity.

Diego smiled. "I'm sure it will, Uncle."

He patted Diego's hand. "We have a lot to talk about, so I hope you'll stay for a few days. This is an interesting area which fortunately hasn't been discovered by too many tourists yet. The locals are trying their hardest to attract them, by opening rural lodgings and suchlike, but we're so isolated that I trust it will never become too popular."

"But they might be good for business; your business, I mean," said Frank, and in view of what we were soon to discover about his work, it was remarkable that he didn't wince, but Abelardo had more poise than anyone I'd ever met before.

"Tourism is a double-edged sword," he said. "While it might inject some life into Fermoselle and stop the population from falling still further, it can make people greedy and cause them to neglect their traditional pursuits. I saw this during the three months I spent on Lanzarote some time ago."

"I thought you just went there on holiday," said Diego.

He smiled. "Yes, a long holiday. It reinvigorated my painting, but on the whole I prefer the light here. I paint landscapes for pleasure and portraits to make a little money. Come, I'll show you your rooms and my studio."

After walking up the tiled staircase Diego and I immediately told Frank that he could have the small single room, as we'd got used to sharing and preferred not to take a fifty-fifty gamble on being subjected to his midnight discourses. In our bigger room with twin beds there were two marvellous landscape paintings on the walls, but in Abelardo's austere room which he showed us there were none. On reaching the next floor we entered a completely different world. Apart from a small storeroom, it was an airy, open space illuminated by huge double glazed windows. Before we had time to take in the paraphernalia of a well-organised artist's studio, Abelardo led us up some more stairs onto a terrace with magnificent views of the village and the wooded river gorge to the west. From the railings to the rear we even caught a glimpse of the Duero reflecting the sun that had finally come out.

"I sometimes paint up here, but mostly in the studio," he said.

"This is a fantastic place," said Frank.

"I like it. I bought it very cheaply about fifteen years ago and spent a long time doing it up, with some help from a local builder."

I gazed at the rooftops falling away towards the plains to the east, then back at the verdant ravine which seemed ever so close but was in fact about a mile away. "Are houses here still cheap?"

"I know prices rose, then fell again, but right now I'm not sure," he said slowly and clearly. He smiled. "Why, do you like it here, Justin?"

"It's wonderful."

"But very cold in winter. Not as cold as on the plains, because of its lower altitude and the river valley, but cold enough. Then again, it's cold in Ólvega too."

Diego stopped smiling for the first time since we'd arrived. "I doubt there's much to do here though."

Abelardo smiled. "That's true in the sense that few entertainments are provided, but the people are friendly and if one has interests to keep oneself occupied, life can be very pleasant. The nearest city is Zamora, sixty-five kilometres away, and in between there is only one small town of a similar size to this one. We are truly isolated here."

"How many people live here?" I asked.

"Now, about twelve hundred. Until the 1950s there were over four thousand, then the emigration began. The same story as in Soria and many other places."

"But not Ólvega," I said before Diego could.

"No, even when I was there it was a remarkable place."

"Is there any industry here?" Diego asked.

"Hardly any at all."

"It'll have to be tourism then."

"I don't really mind. It won't bother me here. Come, I'll show you the painting I'm working on now, then I expect you'll wish to rest for a while."

Abelardo was putting the finishing touches to a large portrait of an elegant middle-aged lady with excellent bone structure, as Frank pointed out.

The artist chuckled. "Yes, the face is slightly less plump than that of the lady herself. Almost imperceptibly so, in fact, but those little details please my clients. It doesn't do to be overly flattering, but they always desire marginal improvements."

"Who is she?" Diego asked.

"Oh, the wife of a wealthy man from Salamanca. She came to sit about three weeks ago, but I also work from photographs. I find this one quite satisfactory, and of course it will help to pay the bills."

One glance at Frank told me that he was dying to ask him how much he charged, so I was relieved when Diego asked first.

Abelardo smiled. "It varies a lot. Over the years I've slowly learnt to become a shrewd businessman, although it isn't really in my nature. As this one is the first I've done for the Salamanca elite, I've come to an understanding with the lady's husband. I will only charge him €7000, but he has agreed to insinuate that the price was somewhat higher. This suits us both, of course, and may lead to more work."

Frank whistled. "That's a good amount."

"It isn't at all excessive and I don't paint so many portraits, perhaps half a dozen a year."

Diego grinned. "And how much do you charge the bigwigs from Madrid?"

He smiled. "Come, I'll show you a landscape I'm working on."

He turned an easel away from the wall to reveal an unfinished picture of a volcano with a lake and icy mountains in the background.

"That isn't around here," said Frank.

"Ha, no, it's the Viti Crater at Askja in Iceland. I spent a month there in the spring. I made many sketches and took hundreds of photographs, so now I entertain myself by making paintings."

"So do you never sell the landscapes?" said Diego.

He smiled at Frank and me. "My nephew has a strong commercial instinct. I used to sell the odd one when times were harder, but now I usually give them away. I suppose it's one way of being remembered here when I die, assuming they keep them."

"So when did you make painting your work, Uncle?"

He told us that after deciding to stay in the town he'd rented a tiny house and set up shop as a private tutor, teaching English, Spanish grammar, maths and whatever else the less gifted students required to enable them to move on to the next course at school. After a year or so he'd taken up drawing again, having been a dab hand at it as a boy, and had soon progressed to watercolours and finally oils.

"It was just a hobby for a long time. I taught myself conventional painting, then dabbled with more abstract methods, before realising that it wasn't for me. I lived from hand to mouth here for three or four years. I didn't have a car and I sometimes couldn't even afford to go to the bar for a drink, so when the former mayor commissioned a portrait and offered to pay me the princely sum of seven hundred euros, I jumped at the chance." He shrugged. "He liked it, so little by little I got more and better commissions."

"Why didn't you tell me this, Uncle? I thought you were still teaching."

He smiled. "I still teach occasionally, but I no longer charge. You must not have asked me about the remunerative side of my painting, or I'd have told you."

"No, I was probably moaning about Blackburn and Emma."

He chuckled. "I'm glad you've come home now. Lancashire wasn't for you, but at least you've experienced a different place and made two fine friends there."

I smiled and Frank shrugged modestly.

"Have you got a website?" Diego asked.

"I don't even have a computer, and only a simple mobile phone. Although I do use the internet at the library occasionally, I dislike technology, so I try to do without it."

"But you have a car," said Diego.

"Yes, it's hard to get around without one here. I think my next one will be electric, if I can be sure of getting to Barajas without being stranded," he said, referring to the main Madrid airport. "Now I'm going to have a short siesta. Feel free to do likewise or explore the town. Come down and I'll give you a key."

Diego opted for a snooze, so Frank and I went out to have a look around. Being a medieval town which has suffered little development, Fermoselle has many venerable old buildings, a few quaint arches, several steep cobbled streets, and at least four *miradores*, or viewing points, which have been embellished to please the tourists. We saw some of them ambling around, all Spanish, mainly in the vicinity of the ruined castle and the main church. The best viewing point was at the end of the old town, just past the castle remains, where a few people were taking photos of the sliver of river that could be seen. Frank and I hadn't spoken much as we toured the town, preferring to take it all in and, I think, reflect on the intelligence, modesty and almost monk-like serenity of our host.

I asked Frank if he was thinking of doing any filming.

"Oh, I suppose I may do a bit at some point."

"You don't sound too keen."

"Abelardo might not like it if I bother the locals. I've got a feeling that he likes to keep a low profile. I could interview some tourists, I suppose, though I doubt they'll have anything interesting to say." He pointed at a couple wearing walking shoes. "I believe there are some good walking routes around here, so we could do a few morning hikes and let Diego spend some time with his uncle."

"And when we leave here?"

"Back towards Ólvega, I think, maybe stopping off along the way. We can save Galicia for another time, unless you really want to go now."

"I'm easy."

"Back in Diego's dream town I guess we could start looking into finding a place to rent, or places, if you prefer to live alone," he said with unusual solicitude, making me think that a little of Abelardo's finesse had already rubbed off on him.

"It'd be daft and uneconomical not to share, so we could look for a biggish place where we'll each have our own space," I said, realising that I'd just committed myself to something that I might live to regret.

A smile played on his lips. "We'll see what's on offer. There's no hurry, so if we don't find anything, Diego can put the word out while we're back home winding up our affairs."

"Winding up our affairs," I echoed, feeling a tingling sensation in my arms. "I still can't quite believe it's going to happen."

"Oh, it's going to happen all right. Nothing ventured, nothing gained, and neither of us has any commitments. If anything you're in a better position because of your bookkeeping opportunities. I'll have to find some classes, but I don't mind. It'll be a good way to get to know more folk, maybe even a cute divorcee whose kid I'll have to get through his exams."

I looked round at the village. "It's nice here, isn't it?"

"It's picturesque, yes."

"In some ways I'd prefer to live here than in Ólvega."

He chuckled. "Don't be impulsive, Justin. You know nothing about the place, and remember, Ólvega may just be our launchpad to the rest of the north. We'll spend the winter there, then each of us can decide whether to move on or not."

I laughed and shook my head. "Frank, a few hours ago you were your usual temperamental self, and now you seem like the most level-headed bloke in the world. What's come over you?"

"One gets older and wiser with each passing hour."

"You don't. I think Abelardo's civilising influence has already affected you."

"Nonsense. Come on, let's have a drink and kill some time. We oughtn't to butt in just yet. They'll have a lot of catching up to do and they won't want us around."

"That's very considerate of you."

"Just common sense."

Then I caught a reassuring flash of the old Frank.

"Ooh, look, that old chap's got a walking stick like some of the pilgrims we saw in Astorga. I believe there are more routes to Santiago, so this place must be on one of them. Look at the size of his rucksack. He must be a hardcore pilgrim, camping out every night. Damn it, if I'd brought my camera I'd have nabbed him."

"Nip back for it. It won't take you five minutes and I won't let him out of my sight."

His eyes gradually dimmed. "No, he looks a bit stern and pious. If I upset him, word might get back to Abelardo."

"Suit yourself."

Back at the same bar in the square I searched for properties to rent in Ólvega, but was disappointed to find only one flat on offer in the whole town.

"Word of mouth will be more effective," said Frank. "I bet folk prefer to rent them on the sly so as not to declare the income."

I looked at my phone. "There are tons of places in Soria though; the city, I mean. You know, we haven't even been there yet." I googled it. "Forty thousand inhabitants. That's a third of the size of Blackburn. We'll definitely have to go and have a look. We'd only be thirty miles from Ólvega, and you'd get tons of classes if you wanted them."

Frank sipped his *sin alcohol*, then tutted and shook his head as if at a wayward child. "Justin, what's got into you? Your thoughts seem to be flying in all directions. First Ólvega, then here, and now Soria. There's no hurry, so just try to chill out and enjoy the present. The future will take care of itself."

"Yes, Frank. I shall attempt to rein in my impetuosity."

"You do that."

On our return at about half past seven, Abelardo and Diego were in the sitting room, looking at photos.

"Hola, my uncle's been all over the place in the last few years. Iceland, Turkey, Vietnam, Kazakhstan, Ethiopia, Finland… and he still takes photos on one of those old film cameras."

"You choose unusual places," I said.

"Yes, I prefer to avoid tourists, which wasn't possible in Iceland, but the scenery made up for it."

Diego passed the photos around and I saw there weren't many of each place, but they were all good ones. Apart from a few human dots in the distance, there were no people in them.

"So have you painted all these places?" I asked, not quite so correctly, as my grammar lagged behind my comprehension, although, as I said earlier, Frank has helped me to reconstruct many of our conversations.

"Yes, but some more than others. I don't always travel expressly to find good landscapes, but to see different cultures. I try to meet some local people whenever possible, with someone who can translate for me, of course."

"But you haven't taken any photos of them."

Hs smiled. "I've taken a few, but I'll show you those another time. Each of those pictures tells a story and I don't wish to bore you with tales of my travels." He chuckled. "I much prefer to listen than to talk."

"Frank makes films," I said.

"Really? That *is* interesting. What kind of films have you made?"

Spurred on by his curiosity, Frank proceeded to describe his exploits to date, downplaying any silliness and truthfully stressing that he was a mere novice. Aberardo smiled and nodded throughout his surprisingly self-effacing summary.

"You've done a lot in a short time, Frank, and you must keep it up. There are no citizens with exceptional achievements in Fermoselle, but if you wish to interview another mayor you could do so with ours. He too is fond of being filmed. There's also a German enologist called Jorge who planted a vineyard near here a few years ago. He appeared on regional television once, I believe. Other than them... well, I'm going to invite you to dinner at a favourite restaurant of mine now, so someone else might occur to me."

"He could interview you, Uncle."

He smiled. "No, I've never been interviewed and I don't mean to start now. I'll work behind the scenes during your time here, Frank."

Frank beamed and must have flicked on the light switch behind his eyeballs, because it was clear that his filming fervour had been reignited.

"Oh, muchísimas gracias, Abelardo! I didn't wish to bore you with my inconsequential little pastime, but it's true that I have –

like you when you began painting, no doubt – more serious aspirations for the future. I know I have a tough road ahead of me, but I feel sure that with the encouragement of my friends I'll be able to develop the modicum of talent which I believe I possess and eventually, after many years of tireless labour, become a gr... competent film-maker."

During the latter part of this stream of babble I observed Abelardo's face, but saw not a single tensed muscle, let alone the twitches or spasms that a lesser man would have suffered on being subjected to this sudden outpouring.

He just smiled. "You speak excellent Spanish, Frank."

"Gracias, Abelardo."

"And you have great drive, no doubt. When I began painting I had no such belief in myself, and only very slowly did it dawn on me that I might one day achieve a certain proficiency."

I glanced at the Domínguez picture that his proficiency had helped him to acquire.

"Yes, yes, I feel that way too, Abelardo," the little sycophant drawled. "Ha, but one lives in hope, doesn't one?"

"Indeed one does." He glanced at his modest watch. "We'll leave shortly to be sure of getting a table."

Frank sprang to his feet. "Shall I... shall I bring my camera?"

He smiled. "No, Frank, I'd rather you didn't."

The restaurant was on the main street towards the newer part of town. A plump woman in her forties ushered us to a table by the window and chided Abelardo for having stayed away for so long.

"I'm sorry, Mar, but I've been working hard on a commission. This is Diego, my nephew, and Frank and Justin, his friends from England."

She nodded at us and beamed at Diego. "So you have come at last."

"Yes, at last."

"Mar runs the best restaurant in town, like her mother and grandmother before her. It's a true matriarchal line, is it not, Mar?"

She shrugged. "That's the way it's worked out."

Meanwhile Frank's eyes were shifting repeatedly between Mar and Abelardo's faces and I feared a premature interruption.

"Hold your horses," I murmured.

While Mar was getting our drinks Abelardo recommended the steak with duck's liver or the cod with ratatouille, and as we nibbled at a few tapas the place began to fill up, largely with locals, it being a Friday night. Many of them greeted Abelardo and some came over to exchange a few words. They treated him with a certain reverence and Diego asked him if he'd begun to feel like a Fermosellano after so many years.

"Not really. I trust I'll always be considered a welcome outsider here. It's a close-knit community which swells enormously during the fiestas next month, when thousands of emigrants come home."

"Thousands?" I said.

"Yes, for many decades people have had to leave to make a living elsewhere, but they remain attached to the town. Ha, there are now third generation emigrants who still feel that this is their true home."

I asked him if any moved back after retiring, but he believed that as few came back as Ólvegueños returned to their villages.

"They love to come in summer, but in their hearts they know they wouldn't wish to live here again." He chuckled. "They've become too used to what passes for civilisation."

"What are the fiestas like?" Frank asked.

"Crowded and long. They erect a wooden bullring in the square and have *encierros* there. For the last eleven years I've gone on a trip at that time, as it's just too noisy for me." He chuckled. "When they begin to erect the bullring, people ask me when I'll be off."

"Where are you going this year?" Frank asked.

"To Norway. I'm always drawn to the north in summer, partly to escape the heat."

"Ah, when I'm... if I'm ever a successful film-maker, I'd love to travel around the world, making documentaries."

Abelardo smiled. "It's good when one's dreams lie within one's profession."

"Oh, sí."

"Would you like to interview Mar? I think she'll be willing."

"Oh, sí."

"And the mayor? That's him over there."

"Oh, sí."

"And I could call Jorge, the German winemaker, if you like."

"Oh, sí, gracias, Abelardo."

"Would you like to do some long walks?" I murmured to Diego in English.

"Oh, yes, thanks, Justin."

Abelardo glanced over at a table in the corner. "And then there's... but I suppose you have enough interviewees now, Frank."

Frank stared over my shoulder.

"Please don't stare, Frank," said Abelardo. "The large, older man is called Arsenio. He's from a nearby village and he used to travel all over Spain as a picador."

"The picadors are the men who stick their spears into the bulls from their horses," Frank told me in English.

"I know that," I replied in Spanish.

"Do you think he'd give me an interview?" he asked Abelardo.

"I'm not sure. He's a reserved man. He was never very well-known, you know, and usually worked at the smaller bullrings, but he has some interesting stories, if you know how to draw him out."

"Oh, yes, I think I'll know how to do that now."

I observed the big brown balding man as he speared a piece of tomato with consummate skill. He was talking and smiling, but I saw unmistakable signs of irascibility on his face. A little warning bell sounded in my head.

"Er, Frank, I wouldn't bother with him, if I were you," I said in English.

"Oh, I have a hunch that he'll be the best of the lot."

"I have a hunch that it won't end well, and we don't want that to happen here, do we?"

"If he agrees to be interviewed, you must try to remain objective and avoid the typical questions about the cruelty of the bullfight," Abelardo said in Spanish. "That way he may open up and tell you some interesting stories, but if you do as modern interviewers tend to do, in order to try to please the general public, he will become annoyed and your meeting may end acrimoniously."

Frank shook his head and smiled. "You don't need to worry about that, Abelardo. I've perfe… improved my technique during my last interviews and I feel sure that I'll know how to get the best out of him."

I found these final words a little ambiguous, so I suggested he show Abelardo the films he'd made so far. "Including the one with Señor Revilla."

He smiled. "I've exported them all to that cloud thingy and erased them to free up space."

I believed him. "I see."

"Yes, I consider all that stuff to be my apprenticeship." He glanced at Abelardo. "Or rather my early apprenticeship. This second stage will be more professional, as I'll have learnt from my mistakes."

Abelardo nodded. "I'll have a word with them shortly. Will you be available at any time?"

"Oh, yes. I'm at their disposal."

We took our time over coffee so that Abelardo wouldn't have to interrupt the mayor and the picador until they got theirs. When he stood up, Frank asked him if he ought to come along.

"That won't be necessary, Frank."

He approached the mayor, a thickset man in his sixties, who glanced over and soon gave him the nod. Arsenio the picador appeared to need a bit more cajoling, but Abelardo soon told us that we could drive over to his village on Tuesday morning. The mayor would receive Frank at the town hall at ten o'clock sharp on Monday, and after Abelardo had paid the bill Mar agreed to spare Frank half an hour in the afternoon.

"Muchas gracias, Abelardo," Frank said as we strolled back along the cool, almost deserted street. "That just leaves the German winemaker."

"I'll call him tomorrow. If he agrees you'll probably have to go to his bodega, but I'll tell you how to find it."

"Thanks. Oh, but won't you be coming along?"

Abelardo told him that as he needed to finish the portrait within a week or so, he'd take the opportunity to work while we were out. I took the hint and told him that Diego and I were keen to explore the countryside. He said he'd recommend some good routes and soon after arriving home we all retired to our rooms. That night the midnight discourse I'd hoped to avoid happened anyway, because a while after we'd switched off the light Frank slipped into our room and sat on my bed.

"Diego?" I said, a little confused.

"It's me," he murmured.

I groaned and flicked on the bedside light. "What do you want?" I whispered. "You'll wake Diego."

"No, he won't," said he.

I looked at Frank for the first time and rather than the happy, eager, tiresome face I'd expected, I saw a sad frown.

"You were joking about going walking weren't you?" he said.

"Of course not. We want to see the river gorge and whatever else there is around here."

His head fell. "Oh, I see, right. Fair enough."

"You don't need us anyway. You've managed very well alone up to now, haven't you?"

He shrugged. "My interviews in Astorga were all right, but they were just tourists and local kids. Here I thought I might be able to count on a little moral support, but I see I was mistaken." He sighed and stood up. "Night."

"Night, Frank."

"I'll come to your first one with the mayor," said Diego.

He smiled. "Thanks, Diego. I knew I could count on you."

I recalled that Mar had promised him just half an hour. "I'll come with you to the restaurant then."

"Thanks, Justin."

"And we'll see about the others. Goodnight."

"Yes, goodnight." He sat down. "This would be a great place to make a short film, wouldn't it?"

"Oh, God," I moaned.

"It's such a good setting, and after I've proven myself with the interviews I bet lots of folk will be up for a spot of acting."

Diego sat up. "I was going to tell you something tomorrow, but I think now might be a good time."

Suspenseful silence.

"Well?" Frank said.

"I'd like to head home from here. I know it's only been three weeks, but I'm... well, I guess I'm getting a bit homesick. My mum's concerned that I should start looking for a job soon too. You can stay at our flat for as long as you like, of course, or if you want to visit Galicia I could drive you up there."

"Fear not," said Frank. "Our wanderlust isn't inexhaustible either, and it's always better to leave something for later."

"Galicia can wait for now," I said.

"Yes, we'll do what has to be done here, then toddle off back."

I sensed ambiguity again.

"But no short film, Frank, just the interviews. We don't want to outstay our welcome and we can always come back another time."

He patted my leg. "We'll see. Goodnight then."

"Night, Frank." I reached for the light switch.

"Of course, one thing we could do is–"

We heard what sounded like a deliberate cough through the wall, so Frank tiptoed out.

15

It turned out that the enologist was on holiday in Germany, but Frank seemed satisfied with his three appointments and didn't bug us much that weekend as we did our morning walks and mooched around the village until lunchtime, when Abelardo knocked off work. On Saturday we walked to an ancient hermitage and from there to the *Mirador de las Escaleras* viewing point, where we saw a majestic bend of the river which would eventually reach the sea at Porto. From there we followed a rough path through scrub and small trees until the heat drove us back to town. On Sunday morning we fancied a trip abroad, so we drove the ten miles to Bemposta, a neat but unremarkable Portuguese village, before taking a walk to view the river from that side. Back in the village we drank a *cerveja* apiece – *sem álcool* for Frank, of course – in a very quiet bar, then drove back over the dam that Frank opined was Spain's way of squeezing every last drop from the river before they left their poor little neighbour with the dregs.

Over lunch back at the house Abelardo pointed out that the river continued to form the frontier for another sixty kilometres to the south and that a joint hydrographical plan ensured that the Portuguese received sufficient water. I asked him if there was much social exchange across the border and he said that since the once flourishing smuggling industry had finally died out after the

Schengen Agreement of 1985 there wasn't much toing and froing at all.

"I believe Spain has always lived with its back to Portugal, so apart from a few tourists we see little of them nowadays." He chuckled. "When I first arrived here I expected the villagers to speak a little Portuguese, but they had next to no interest in their neighbours. I believe this is the case all the way along the border, with just a few exceptions. It's a pity in a way, but relations between the two countries were uneasy for centuries, so it might be a case of the prejudices of the ruling classes permeating the rest of society."

Abelardo was full of titbits of information like this and he did eventually show us the photos of the people he'd met and conversed with in Kazakhstan, Vietnam, Lapland and Anatolia in Turkey. He spoke about them only briefly, but I sensed that he had many a tale to tell, so I suggested that he might want to write a book about his travels one day.

"Ah, were life not so brief I might consider that, but now that my economic situation is more comfortable I wish to concentrate on my art. I still have much to learn about landscape painting and I'm intrigued by some contemporary artists who incorporate abstract elements in their work." He smiled. "We can't just continue to emulate your great Constable, Turner and Gainsborough *ad infinitum*, after all. I'm in touch with a Swedish artist called Andreas Eriksson. He paints remarkable pictures and has offered to give me some tuition at his house in the country. I suspect this won't be cheap, so I think I'll paint a few more portraits before arranging the visit, maybe next year."

I glanced at Frank, who appeared to be mesmerised by our host.

"So after all these years, you're still learning," I said.

"Oh, yes, one never ceases to learn. Those who think they've acquired mastery in their field often prove to be mediocrities, no matter how popular they may be at the time. People are easily seduced by success and adulation. This is why I prefer to resist the temptation to use the internet to promote my work. I suppose I'm vain enough to wish to be remembered, but I've no desire to become well-known now." He chuckled. "Who knows? It might go to my head."

"I too wish to keep a low profile for the time being," said Frank. "A lot of so-called film-makers put everything they do on YouTube, but I shan't be doing that."

"I bet you will if you think you can make some money out of it," said Diego.

I wondered if the video of the naked Andoni might go viral. I doubted the big Basque would be pleased if it did, but then again he might be.

Frank tutted. "No, no, instant gratification of that kind is of no interest to me," he said, his intonation becoming uncannily similar to Abelardo's.

"I once read a theory that one needs to spend ten thousand hours carrying out an activity in order to become proficient at it," said Abelardo. "When I reflected on this and made some calculations I was inclined to agree with the figure, although I think fifteen or twenty thousand might be nearer the mark."

Frank's frowning face indicated that he was making a few calculations of his own. "Er, that's a lot of hours behind the camera."

Abelardo's merry laugh suggested that Frank really tickled him. "Behind the camera, directing, writing, rehearsing, planning, reading all you can about film-making; all those things count, Frank. Ten thousand hours is about five years of full-time work. After ten years of painting I began to feel that I was getting somewhere, but don't let these figures put you off. Just take it day by day and learn from your mistakes."

Frank rubbed his hands together. "I can't wait to get stuck in tomorrow."

Yet more ambiguity, I thought.

Over lunch on Monday Diego told us that the mayor had lost no time into getting stuck into telling Frank all about Fermoselle and his role in making it a dynamic, thrusting tourist centre. The man really was 'Mr Fermoselle', and the fact that his surname was Fermoselle had done him no harm at all during his frequent TV interviews. On viewing the footage we saw him rabbiting on for about twenty minutes with next to no prompting from Frank.

"I'm not sure that even counts towards my ten thousand hours," he said glumly.

"Of course it does," said Abelardo. "The sound and the lighting are good and you did exactly what you had to do. He never really strayed from the point, so you were right to stay silent. A lesser interviewer would have butted in just to show that he was in charge, but you resisted that temptation. Well done."

Frank blushed becomingly.

"Now, I suspect that Mar may wish to talk more about recipes than the interesting history of her restaurant, so I suggest that you subtly keep her on track, unless you want recipes, of course."

"Oh, no, I want to dig much deeper than that."

"Don't dig, just prompt," I said sagely.

I fulfilled my promise to lend him moral support and was impressed by what I saw. Mar wished to be interviewed in the kitchen, but Frank insisted on seating her by a window in the empty restaurant where the light was good and the background attractive. Before filming he pleased her by expressing earnest interest in the history of the place, and once they'd begun he kept her on track by means of a few pertinent comments whenever she tried to go off on a recipe-inspired tangent. After the allotted half hour was up she cheerfully bade us goodbye until our next visit.

"That was really good, Frank," I said as we wandered back to the square. "Professional enough to be seen on TV, I'd say."

He shrugged. "Hmm, regional TV maybe. I thought it went quite well, but I'm sure I'll find plenty of things to improve when I view it. Hopefully Abelardo will be able to give me a few pointers."

"But he isn't a film-maker."

"Art is art, and he's a true artist. A man like him could turn his hand to anything."

I chuckled. "It seems funny now that you once called him a monster."

He came to a halt. "What? Oh, right. Bah, the lad must have been the devil incarnate to deceive him like that, and he was a much younger man then. I suppose the scheming sod might have inspired him aesthetically, before he saw the error of his ways."

"Yes, when he'd emptied his wallet and run off."

Frank shook his head. "Do try to rise above these petty prejudices, Justin. We've all committed mistakes in the past and they help us to become the more well-rounded people we are today."

I had no answer to that, so we went back to the house, where Frank's mentor praised his latest effort.

"My only criticism is that you said 'vale' four or five times, Frank." (Vale means OK.) "It's a rather informal word when used in that sense and is often quite redundant. When it isn't, I would say 'de acuerdo' instead."

"De acuerdo, Abelardo," said Frank. "That's just the sort of thing I need to be told about." He glanced at me. "It's fine to say 'that was great', but if I'm ever going to achieve perfection I'll need plenty of constructive criticism."

"I'll take a break tomorrow morning and come along to Arsenio's with you," said Abelardo, causing Frank to grin and blush like a virgin bride.

"Oh, *muchas* gracias, Abelardo. I'm sure you'll be a great help."

So it was that when Frank reached the retired picador's scruffy bungalow the next morning he had his complete entourage in tow. While Abelardo chatted to the interviewee inside, Frank took totally unnecessary light readings on the patio while Diego and I fetched the required chairs and a little table upon which Arsenio was to have a glass of brandy whether he wanted it or not.

"It'll look just right. Oh, I hope Abelardo convinces him."

"To do what?" I said.

He grinned. "You'll see, I hope."

Picadors tend to be heavy men so that they can really stick their lance into the bull's neck, but Arsenio's ornate yellow jacket and lemon-coloured breeches fit him so tightly that he looked fit to burst. He wore a cute little hat too, and carried a *pica*, or lance, which Frank decided to prop against the wall just to the left of him. Arsenio seemed happy enough to be wearing his old work clothes and consented to the glass of brandy that his doctor had told him to abstain from.

"You don't need to drink it," said Abelardo, who'd met him towards the end of his career, when he'd been a boisterous reveller during his time off and a man not to be crossed. Our host had conveyed this information to Frank and I'd repeated it on the way there, just in case.

He took a tiny sip. "For the nerves, you know."

The interview began really well. After speaking briefly and modestly about his long career and some of the more famous bullfighters he'd occasionally worked with, he began to reminisce on the glory days of the picador. Apparently in the olden days the picador had been the star of the show, when he would spear the bull from his unprotected horse as many times as he liked. Back then the *corrida* was all about watching the picador's horsemanship and the matador was merely the minion who finished off the bull when the main man had brought it to its knees. It was all fascinating stuff, but as I watched from behind the camera I found myself dwelling on the extreme cruelty of old-fashioned bullfighting, because not only the bull but also the horse often died after the uneven combat, having had its innards ripped to shreds by the bull's horns.

Frank told me later that day, after all the fuss had died down, that it had been the recollection of a scene from a Hemingway book that had first made him see red. The passage described how in the 1920s the horses would sometimes have their intestines shoved back in before they were stitched up and ridden back into the ring for one last charge. They were put down afterwards and sold for meat.

"But during your time the horses wore protection, didn't they?" was his first ominous enquiry.

Arsenio smiled. "Of course. Since 1928 the horses have worn protection and this has increased in size and thickness over the years. Very few of my horses received serious injuries."

"What? How?"

He chuckled and sipped his brandy. "The *toro de lidia* is a five-hundred-kilogramme beast with sharp horns, young man. The horses often suffer broken ribs and internal injuries, but I believe that they too enjoy the fight, just like the bull."

"Bollocks," Frank muttered in English.

"What's that?" Arsenio enquired.

"Nada. So, you claim that the bulls actually enjoy being... in the ring?"

He smiled. "Of course. They have a wonderful life for three or four years before they finally meet their destiny."

"Their destiny?"

He frowned and took a drink. "Of course. They are bred for the *corrida*. They can sense that one day they will engage in mortal combat. You must remember that the bull enters the ring believing that he can win, and occasionally he does, when he wounds or even kills the matador."

"And what happens then?"

His eyes narrowed. "Have you never attended a *corrida*, young man?"

"Of course not. What happens then?"

"Then another member of the *cuadrilla* finishes off the bull, but in a sense it dies knowing it has been victorious." He finished his brandy and smiled. "Oh, and very occasionally the bull is pardoned. Those privileged animals, if they recover, go on to breed more fine bulls." He frowned. "Since I retired they've begun to pardon more and more bulls; far too many in my opinion."

"So the only good bull's a dead bull then, is it, in *your* opinion?"

Abelardo's deliberate cough had no effect this time, but I saw that he was smiling, so I wasn't too worried, despite the evident ascent of blood to Arsenio's head.

"I invited you here today on the understanding that we were to speak about my career and the art of the picador."

"Art my arse," he mumbled in English. "And I came here with the intention of laying aside my scruples regarding the savage cruelty to which these poor beasts are subjected," he said, looking straight at the camera. "But try as one might, one cannot help but conclude that this *barbarous* activity should be banned right away," he almost shouted, but he had the foresight to lean towards the camera, so when Arsenio lunged at him – without his lance – Frank leapt to his feet, yanked out the mic lead, grabbed the tripod and scuttled off down the track crying, "Savages, murderers, criminals!" while still filming the fuming picador who – unfortunately, Frank later claimed – didn't deign to chase him.

Arsenio sat down and soon stopped panting. "Why did you bring that damned cretin here, Abelardo?"

He managed to keep a straight face. "I'm sorry, Arsenio. He promised to stay off the subject of cruelty, but he must have got carried away."

"He provoked you on purpose," said Diego soothingly. "He's a complete fool sometimes."

Arsenio shrugged and unbuttoned his jacket. "Oh, well, we're used to that type of thing these days. I think I'll have another drop of that brandy."

"Remember your doctor's orders," said Abelardo.

"To hell with the doctor. Come inside out of the sun and we'll all have a little something."

Rather than coming sloping back and humbly apologising, Frank reached the road and set off back to town, assuming that we'd pick him up within a few minutes after the furious picador had bundled his tormentor's sidekicks out of there. In the end he hitched a lift and when he called me about two hours later we'd just left Arsenio's, having discussed the past, present and future of bullfighting very amicably indeed. I'd confessed to a certain aversion to it and Arsenio had said that he understood that, but that one oughtn't to ban a *fiesta* that had been going on for hundreds of years – probably right back to Roman times – just because of a few rabid vegetarians being up in arms about it. When I said I wasn't a vegetarian he went in for the kill – dialectically speaking – by pointing out that the animals I ate, particularly the chickens, led awful, miserable lives, unlike the noble bull who lorded it over his lush pasture and ate the best fodder money could buy.

"Vegetarian fodder," he added, amused by my discomfiture. "Let he who is without sin cast the first stone, eh? Anyway, tell your friend that I'm no longer angry with him, so if I see him in town he won't need to run away."

Abelardo screwed the top onto the brandy bottle. "That's good of you, Arsenio, but if my nephew and our friend have no objections, I plan to teach him a little lesson." He chuckled. "He broke his promise and needs to be punished, I think."

He explained his intentions and Diego and I agreed wholeheartedly. After firm handshakes and a bit of backslapping – Arsenio was as strong as a bull – we said goodbye, collected Frank's abandoned microphone, and drove away in Abelardo's saloon car.

"How's it going?" Frank said breezily when I picked up, Abelardo having already pulled over and ushered me out of the car.

"Fine."

"Ha, what a coup, eh? Being attacked by a furious picador. Shame he didn't chase me."

"Where are you now?"

"In the bar in the square. I did get genuinely angry, you know, but I'm glad now. I've got a great bit of footage."

"I'll come over shortly with your things."

"What things?"

"All of them. Abelardo doesn't want to set eyes on you again. You broke your promise to behave and you've almost ruined a good friendship."

"But..."

"We've been there all this time while Abelardo was trying to patch things up with him. He finally came round a bit, but there'll be no such reconciliation between you and Abelardo, I'm afraid. One of his rules is never to bother with people who break their promises." I clenched my teeth.

"You're joking?"

I unclenched them. "Do I sound like I'm joking, you pillock? You'll have to find a hotel tonight and we'll probably set off home tomorrow, or maybe the next day. You're not exactly flavour of the month with Diego either, so you'll just have to make your own fun till we go."

"I don't believe it."

"Believe it. I'll come to the bar in a... an hour or so. Bye." I hung up and hopped back in the car. "I do believe I'm a born actor," I said in English.

"How did he react?" Abelardo said in Spanish.

"He believed me. Now one hour for him to suffer, then I go to the bar."

"Yes, that'll be long enough," he said. "Then bring him back for lunch and we'll all have a good laugh about it."

"Are you not annoyed at all, Uncle?"

He chuckled. "How can I be? It was wonderful to watch. One of those moments one will always remember. Frank is a singular mixture of the man trying to gain fulfilment and the eternal clown. I've never met anyone quite like him. He fascinates me." We reached the outskirts of town. "Perhaps you ought to go and get him soon, Justin. I don't want him to believe I'm so headstrong for too long."

"It takes a while for things to sink in with Frank. I'll go in an hour."

Diego came along to the bar to witness my gradual revelation of a hoax that Frank himself might have been proud of, but the scene that greeted us brought us to an abrupt halt in the doorway. There he was at a corner table, with *seven* beer bottles in front of him, all but one of them empty. I looked at the owner and he just shook his head and went on wiping the counter. As we approached, Frank saw us and raised his quarter-full bottle.

"Theeere you are!" he slurred. "Jus' having a lickle drinky-poo. Beer's on me." He belched. "Ger 'em in."

"Holy shit," said Diego.

"Bugger," I said, then began to think. It was just an hour since I'd called. Seven bottles. Stereotypical drunken behaviour. I didn't quite buy it, and when I saw the owner smirk I knew for sure. Still, as it appeared to be Hoax Day I saw no reason to enlighten Diego just yet.

"Bloody hell, Frank!" I wailed. "You've stayed off it for almost a year and now you go and do this." Maybe I'd only be any good as a radio actor, because I saw that Frank rumbled me right away.

"Yesh, and now I'm back on it for good. Where's the fun in a life without booze when everyone gets their twisters in a nick 'cause of some p… p… pestilent picador? Ger 'em in, I say! Let's drink and be merry, 'cause tomorrow's nuther day."

"Ha!" Diego cried. "He's having us on, Justin!"

"Really?"

"Pestilent picador my arse!"

Frank smiled soberly. "Well spotted, Diego. Drunks can't alliterate so… admirably."

"And the bottles?" I said.

"Some blokes left, so I asked Pablo to leave them for a while. I was just getting into character when you arrived." He swirled the beer in the bottle. "This one came in especially handy, but not a drop has passed my lips. Shall we adjourn to a clean table?"

"It's almost time for lunch."

"So is Abelardo not annoyed at all? I thought he might be a bit miffed, but I didn't believe the bit about chucking me out, not after I'd thought about for a while."

I just shook my head.

"My uncle's right about him," Diego said to me. "Especially the clown bit. Come on, let's get back."

Frank performed a final stagger for Pedro and the customers' benefit and we left.

16

Frank's tomfoolery seemed to cement his friendship with Abelardo rather than diminish it. After he'd apologised for his semi-spontaneous outburst we watched the footage and cracked up laughing on seeing Arsenio shaking his fist at the jiggling camera. Later Frank invited us to dinner at Mar's restaurant and Diego announced that he wished to go home soon.

"My mother's been working behind the scenes, you see, and she's lined up two interviews for me; one with a logistics company and the other at a big refrigeration place."

"When?" I asked.

"When I get back. The sooner the better really, so they'll see that I'm keen."

"Fair enough," said Frank, glancing at Abelardo as he often did.

"And are you keen?" I said.

"Yes, as long as the salary's good. I don't want to start as a new man, but as one who's gained valuable experience abroad. I hope to be able to use my English. I'll probably visit more companies and see who makes me the best offer. My family has a reputation as hard workers, so I'm sure I'll get something good."

Abelardo cleared his throat. "I spoke to your father this afternoon, Diego."

"Really?"

"Yes, I thought it was about time. I think your mother had already told him you were having a pleasant visit, because we were soon speaking quite naturally. Oh, I now realise more than ever that I should have called long ago, but the years just passed by."

"He could have called you too," said Diego.

"Hmm, yes, but it was really up to me to get in touch after… the way I left. Anyway, I'll be driving over to Ólvega to pay them a visit quite soon."

I remembered that Diego's parents only had one spare room. "I think Frank and me will look for a place to rent and then go home to… prepare," I said.

Frank nodded. "To wind up our affairs, such as they are."

"Uncle, as I'll be seeing you soon, I think we'll leave tomorrow, if that's all right with you guys."

"OK," I said.

Frank glanced at Abelardo. "Fine. How far is it to Ólvega, Diego?"

"About 417 kilometres. Just four hours if I put my foot down."

"Not far at all," he murmured.

I half-expected a midnight visit from Frank, so when he arrived I made room for him on my bed.

"Any news in the last half hour?" said Diego as he laid aside his book.

"Yes, there is actually. I, er… I shan't be coming back with you tomorrow."

"Eh? Why's that?" I said.

"Oh, I asked Abelardo if I could stay for a while longer and he agreed. I suppose I'd like to see if a bit of his seriousness rubs off on me. When I go he'll run me to Zamora and I'll get buses back. I'll stay for a week or so, I guess." He smiled. "He's going to let me interview him, as long as I promise not to show it to anyone yet. That's one promise I won't be breaking. We'll be taking the portrait to Salamanca soon, so I may be able to interview the rich dude there. Abelardo wants me to meet a pal of his in Zamora too. He used to be a cameraman on national TV, so he should be able to give me a few tips."

"It sounds like he's happy for you to stay," said Diego.

I imagined sleeping alone in his sister's old room. "Yes, that sounds good." Something occurred to me and I decided to make a joke of it. "Don't forget that Abelardo's gay, Frank. He might have designs on you."

I was relieved to hear Diego chuckle.

"Don't be stupid. Our friendship is strictly man to man, as in... you know what I mean."

"I was joking, Frank."

"He told me he's been celibate for a long time anyway. He feels that a partner would distract him from his work."

"Maybe you should remain celibate too then," said Diego.

"Yes, well, the girl at the bakery's been giving me the glad eye, so I might... but no, I've no time for that sort of thing right now."

"What's the glad eye?"

"Something that occurs in Frank's head whenever a woman looks at him."

"I still remember Marta," Diego murmured. "I think I'll email her when I've got a job."

"You do that," I said. "Frank, I'll go ahead and look for a place to rent, shall I?"

"Of course."

"My mother will help," said Diego. "She knows everyone."

I yawned. "Off you go now, Frank. Any more news can wait until breakfast."

He went.

"Do you think he'll stay here for long?" Diego asked me.

"You never know with Frank."

Over breakfast Diego and I considered spending a final night in Aranda del Duero, but once we'd said goodbye and hit the road I knew it would never happen. Diego paid little regard to his fuel consumption – 6.4 litres/100km in the end – as he raced across the plains, but on approaching Soria I said that I'd like to stop.

"Aw, we're nearly home now."

"I just want to take a look."

"You'll see it on the left after we pass the industrial estate."

"No, I mean a proper look. We've been driving for over three hours and I'd dying for a piss. Turn off here."

He groaned and indicated. "There isn't all that much to see."

"Just half an hour then."

Soria's typical high-rise suburbs don't lead one to expect much, but when he pulled over beside a park I couldn't believe the size of it.

"And look at all that grass. What a brilliant park for such a small city."

"Yes, it isn't bad, and there's an even bigger one on the outskirts, with a castle that they haven't bothered restoring. It isn't bad down by the river either, but we can come and see that another day, if you like."

"Yes, I would."

After a long pee and a quick drink at a cafe he led me towards the pedestrianised centre and yet more open spaces with a great big fountain, gardens and an impressive museum. On our high-speed tour I saw several old churches, palaces, a convent, a fine *plaza mayor* and other lesser but equally pleasant squares.

"It feels like a cosmopolitan city," I said as we passed some posh shops on our way back to the car.

"Yes, but it isn't really."

"And there aren't too many tourists."

"No, I think a lot of them skip Soria. I suppose it is a bit of a neglected gem really, but I still prefer Ólvega."

"Yes... yes," I said, not wishing to sing Soria's praises too highly. "Let's get back there."

Forty blurry minutes later Ólvega's splendid industrial estate came into view and Diego emitted a little whoop. "Ah, home sweet home! It feels like I've been away for ages."

"Er, you were, for nine years."

"Yes, but once I came back I didn't want to leave again. It's been a great trip though."

"The best I've ever done. Now to think about the future."

Epilogue

Things were much quieter without Frank, but less amusing too, so I won't draw out this account by detailing the ins and outs of our respective quests during the following fortnight. Diego threw himself wholeheartedly into his job search and was so confident of finding a really good one that he put on hold an offer he had from the logistics company. He was a man on a mission, and so was I, except mine bore next to no fruit for a while. Of the three places that Diego's mum helped me to find, two were tiny flats and one a posh chalet which was way above our budget. As Diego was busy I took the bus into Soria on Friday and spent the morning wandering around the park, the old town and the charming squares. The people seemed pleasant and relaxed, and as I sat on a cafe terrace drinking coffee I could easily see myself living there. I performed a quick search of properties for rent and saw that it would have to be a flat, but there was a great deal of choice. Prices started at only €350 a month, but one spacious enough for Frank and me would cost at least €500. I thought about calling him, but decided to wait until after the weekend.

On Friday and Saturday nights we went out with Diego's friends and the conversations tended to revolve around work, money, cars and suchlike. While chatting to one young chap alone I said that I was torn between living there or in Soria. To my surprise he urged me to go to the city, as there was more to do and I'd meet a better mix of people.

"Here we work hard all week and it's very dull in winter," he said. "You'd be better off in the city, and you could always come here at the weekends."

"That's true."

On Sunday we went to visit Diego's grandmother in Deza. After spending an agreeable couple of hours chatting we took our leave and strolled around for a while.

Diego chuckled when we passed the curious little bullring. "Do you still fancy living in a place like this?"

"Not really. Although it's hot and sunny now I'm trying to envisage life in winter. I think it'd be a bit boring here."

"Definitely. In Ólvega when it's cold and wet you'll have the swimming pools and sports centre."

"That's true. I think I'll go to Soria again tomorrow."

"You like it there, don't you?"

"Yes."

"I think maybe Frank would too."

"Yes, he might."

"And in some ways I think I'd prefer Frank to live there. I still can't forget his so-called interview with Revilla. Here he'd be bound to upset someone sooner or later, and being such a small place... well, what are your thoughts at the moment?"

"To be honest, I'm leaning towards Soria."

"Go for it then. You'll only be renting, after all." He chuckled. "You must come to visit often and in time you'll begin to discover the joys of my town."

"Yes, it might be best to keep Frank away from here. I wonder how he's getting on."

"Well, my uncle hasn't called to report any catastrophes yet, so he must be behaving."

"I'll give him a call tomorrow."

On Monday after locating a couple of theoretically suitable flats I called him from a bar in the park.

"How's it going, Justin, my man?"

"Fine. I'm in Soria. How are you?"

"Great. We're just about to shove the portrait in the car and shoot off to Salamanca. Me and Arsenio are bosom buddies now, by the way."

"Oh, good."

"Yes, we met at Mar's and had a good laugh about my antics. He wants to take me to a bullfight and explain the art of *tauromaquia* to me, but Abelardo advised him not to. He said they might lynch me if I shot my mouth off. Ha, all good fun!"

I told him that I felt inclined to rent a flat in Soria and briefly explained why.

"Hmm, yes, I see what you mean."

"Shall I view some then?"

"Er, yes, go ahead."

I detected uncertainty in his voice. "What are your plans, Frank?"

"Well, although Abelardo and I are getting on like a house on fire, he has pointed out that he doesn't want me under his roof indefinitely. He likes his solitude, you see. I'll look after the place while he's in Norway though."

"And then?"

"Well, to be honest I'm beginning to like Fermoselle a lot. The Arsenio story's got around, mainly because he's been telling it, and they already see me as something of a character. I think they'll give me a bit of leeway here, whereas in Ólvega I'd feel I had to behave myself all the time. As for Soria, I like the idea more, but, well… what do you think?"

I thought about a neat-looking two-bedroom flat not far from the lovely *Parque del Castillo* which would cost me a little over €400 a month. I thought about my need to have quiet working hours in order to earn my bread at the computer. I thought the 370 kilometres that separated Soria from Fermoselle wasn't all that far on quiet Spanish dual-carriageways.

"Are you still there, Justin?"

"Yes. Yes, by all means give it a go in Fermoselle if that's what you want. I think I'll rent a small place here with a spare bedroom, so you'll be able to visit."

"Brilliant."

"But not live there. I can't afford to spend another hundred a month just in case you have a change of heart, so think it over."

"I'm already looking into houses. There are quite a few for rent. A couple of people have expressed interest in classes too, for their kids." He chuckled. "They're getting used to me wandering around with my camera now. In an isolated place like this I think they crave novelty, and I'm the man to give it to them."

"Good. Look, I won't sign anything before Friday, so you have until Thursday night to change your mind."

"All right, but I don't think I will. You could always come to live here, of course. Do you not fancy that?"

I thought about my future independence in Soria and how I'd pick up the language much more quickly if I were left to my own devices. "Not just now. I'm going to spend the winter in Soria."

He chuckled. "No cooling off period back in Blackburn then?"

"No, I must commit myself, within the week."

"You do that. Won't Diego be annoyed about you forsaking his terrific town?"

"He says not. I'm sure I'll go quite often at the weekends. It'll be the best of both worlds really."

"Ah, who could have foreseen that things would pan out like this when we got off that plane in the rain at Bilbao all those weeks ago?"

"Yes, who'd have thought?" I also recalled our conversation in the cafe on that damp June day back in Blackburn. "Yes, it's been a bit of a life-changing time for me."

"And me. It just goes to show that you have to get off your arse to make things happen."

"Yes." I stood up. "I'm going to see a flat. Speak soon."

"Bye, Justin, and give my regards to Diego."

"Will do. Hasta luego."

"Hasta *pronto*, Justin."

"Sí, Frank. See you soon."

THE END

Printed in Great Britain
by Amazon